Language Acquisition and the Multilingual Ideal

Also available from Bloomsbury

Contemporary Second Language Assessment, edited by Jayanti Veronique Banerjee and Dina Tsagari
Crosslinguistic Influence and Crosslinguistic Interaction in Multilingual Language Learning, edited by Gessica De Angelis, Ulrike Jessner and Marijana Kresic
Japanese Questions: Discourse, Context and Language, by Lidia Tanaka
Second Language Acquisition in Action, by Andrea Nava and Luciana Pedrazzini

Language Acquisition and the Multilingual Ideal

Exploring Japanese Language Learning Motivation

Toshiyuki Nakamura

BLOOMSBURY ACADEMIC
LONDON • NEW YORK • OXFORD • NEW DELHI • SYDNEY

BLOOMSBURY ACADEMIC
Bloomsbury Publishing Plc
50 Bedford Square, London, WC1B 3DP, UK
1385 Broadway, New York, NY 10018, USA
29 Earlsfort Terrace, 2 Dublin, Ireland

BLOOMSBURY, BLOOMSBURY ACADEMIC and the Diana logo are trademarks of
Bloomsbury Publishing Plc

First published in Great Britain 2019
This paperback edition published in 2021

Copyright © Toshiyuki Nakamura, 2019

Toshiyuki Nakamura has asserted his right under the Copyright, Designs and Patents Act, 1988, to be identified as Author of this work.

For legal purposes the Acknowledgements on p. viii constitute an extension of this copyright page.

All rights reserved. No part of this publication may be reproduced or transmitted in any form or by any means, electronic or mechanical, including photocopying, recording, or any information storage or retrieval system, without prior permission in writing from the publishers.

Bloomsbury Publishing Plc does not have any control over, or responsibility for, any third-party websites referred to or in this book. All internet addresses given in this book were correct at the time of going to press. The author and publisher regret any inconvenience caused if addresses have changed or sites have ceased to exist, but can accept no responsibility for any such changes.

A catalogue record for this book is available from the British Library.

Library of Congress Cataloging-in-Publication Data

Names: Nakamura, Toshiyuki, author.
Title: Language acquisition and the multilingual ideal: exploring Japanese language learning motivation / Toshiyuki Nakamura.
Description: New York, NY: Bloomsbury Academic, 2019. | Includes bibliographical references and index. |
Identifiers: LCCN 2019020680 (print) | LCCN 2019021661 (ebook) |
ISBN 9781350088160 (epdf) | ISBN 9781350088177 (epub) | ISBN 9781350088153 (hb)
Subjects: LCSH: Japanese language–Study and teaching. | Multilingualism. | Bilingualism.
Classification: LCC PL519 (ebook) | LCC PL519.N3115 2019 (print) | DDC 495.6071–dc23
LC record available at https://lccn.loc.gov/2019020680

ISBN: HB: 978-1-3500-8815-3
PB: 978-1-3502-4448-1
ePDF: 978-1-3500-8816-0
eBook: 978-1-3500-8817-7

Typeset by Newgen KnowledgeWorks Pvt. Ltd., Chennai, India

To find out more about our authors and books visit www.bloomsbury.com and sign up for our newsletters.

Contents

List of figures		vi
List of tables		vii
Acknowledgements		viii
List of abbreviations		ix
1	Introduction	1
2	Understanding language learning motivation 'multilingually'	11
3	'Japanese is easy but difficult to continue.' Motivation and future self-images of Korean learners	29
4	'Japanese is difficult, but I don't want to stop.' Motivation and future self-images of Australian learners	51
5	'I think that English is the first, and the next is Japanese.' Motivational trajectories of Korean learners	79
6	'I really, really want to do Japanese translating.' Motivational trajectories of Australian learners	105
7	Language learning motivation in English-speaking and non-English-speaking contexts	133
Appendix 1(a): First round interview questions (Australian version)		155
Appendix 1(b): First round interview questions (Korean version)		158
Appendix 2(a): Second round interview questions (Australian version)		161
Appendix 2(b): Second round interview questions (Korean version)		163
References		165
Index		173

Figures

7.1 Development of ideal Japanese self in sustained motivational trajectory — 146
7.2 Development of ideal Japanese self in waning motivational trajectory (Type 1: Achievement of ideal Japanese self) — 148
7.3 Development of ideal Japanese self in waning motivational trajectory (Type 2: Weakening of ideal Japanese self) — 148

Tables

3.1	Background of Korean participants	31
3.2	The Korean participants' reasons to keep studying Japanese at university	35
3.3	The Korean participants' projected future L2 use	44
4.1	Background of Australian participants	52
4.2	The Australian participants' reasons to keep studying Japanese at university	59
4.3	The Australian participants' projected future L2 use	73
5.1	The Korean participants' Japanese-related experiences and changes in perceived competence/confidence in the language	80
5.2	Shifts in the Korean participants' projected future L2 use	82
5.3	Korean participants' projected future use of Japanese, future learning intentions, and self-evaluation on motivation	84
5.4	Types of motivational trajectories of the Korean participants	87
6.1	The Australian participants' Japanese-related experiences and changes in perceived competence/confidence in the language	106
6.2	Shifts in the Australian participants' projected future L2 use	109
6.3	Australian participants' projected future use of Japanese, future learning intentions, and self-evaluation on motivation	110
6.4	Types of motivational trajectories of the Australian participants	112

Acknowledgements

In presenting this book for publication, I wish to express my sincere gratitude to the many people who have made it possible.

First, I would like to thank Dr Robyn Spence-Brown and Dr Naomi Kurata for their valuable suggestions and advice. Robyn, your insight always helped me rethink important issues that I initially overlooked. And Naomi, as a Japanese researcher at an Australian university, you have been a role model for my 'ideal self', which has motivated me to research.

I express my appreciation to the Korean and Australian participants who allowed me to conduct interviews. This research project would not have been possible without them, and I am most grateful for their trust. I can only hope that I have presented their lives justly throughout this book.

Finally, I wish to thank my loving family for all their support and patience during my extended preoccupation. A special word of gratitude is due to my awesome wife, Yurong, for her considerable encouragement and self-sacrifice over the years. I am also grateful to my beloved daughter, Sakura. Your kind words have always kept me motivated.

Abbreviations

DST	Dynamic Systems Theory
JET	Japan Exchange and Teaching Program
JLPT	Japanese Language Proficiency Test (a worldwide Japanese government-sponsored test to evaluate proficiency in Japanese of non-native speakers)
JPT	Japanese Proficiency Test (a Japanese-language test organized by a Korean private enterprise, widely accepted in Korean universities)
LOTE	Language Other Than English
N1	the highest certificate of JLPT
SLA	Second Language Acquisition
TOEIC	Test of English for International Communication

1

Introduction

Why study motivation to learn Japanese?

Motivation is considered to be one of the most important individual variables in determining long-term second language (L2) learning success. Because of its importance, numerous researchers in the field of second language acquisition (SLA) have examined learners' motivation, commencing with Gardner and Lambert's (1959) pioneering study. However, L2 motivation is also particularly challenging to theorize and research as scholars have not yet clearly answered the question of what leads a learner to make certain choices, to engage in learning and to persist in action. Since Dörnyei (2005) proposed his motivation theory, the L2 Motivational Self System, learner's L2 self (self-image as a second language user) has been considered to play a central role in L2 learning motivation. That is, language learners' visions of their desirable future selves as competent L2 users can be powerful driving forces of learning motivation as they prompt learners to try to reduce the discrepancy between these visions and their current state.

Research concerning the L2 Motivational Self System have presented significant findings in relation to the mutual relationship between the construction of individuals' L2 selves and their social context (e.g. Kormos, Kiddle and Csizér 2011; Csizér, Kormos and Sarkadi 2010; Kim 2009; Lamb 2009; Huang, Hsu and Chen 2015). However, these studies have mainly focused on learners' motivation for English, as a study (Boo, Dörnyei and Ryan 2015) reported that more than 70 per cent of L2 motivation research was committed to the study of English as a second language during the period between 2005 and 2014. Prominent figures in the field of motivation have, therefore, recently called for more research on the L2 self in languages other than English (LOTEs) (Ushioda and Dörnyei 2017). Another limitation in the research into the L2 Motivational Self System to date has been the lack of attention to cross-linguistic L2 selves. A few studies (Csizér and Dörnyei 2005; Henry

2010, 2011, 2017; Dörnyei and Chan 2013) have investigated the motivational relationship between L2 and L3 self-concepts, including negative impacts of English on learners' self-images in additional languages. However, the complex relationship between different language-specific self-images has not been adequately explored.

Thus, the overall aim of this book is to examine the motivational development of Japanese language learners, in particular, focusing on the development of their future Japanese self-images and their broader self-images as bilingual or multilingual individuals. The four research questions that guided this study were:

1) What are the future L2 self-images of Japanese language learners at various stages of their studies, and how do they relate to their motivation to continue with and invest effort into their study?
2) How are these future self-images and motivation for learning Japanese related to those of other languages?
3) What motivational trajectories can be identified over time, and how do these relate to changes in future self-image?
4) How do contextual factors and individual factors influence motivational trajectories for learning Japanese in two different contexts (Australia and South Korea)?

The first question is of interest because Japanese language learners' motivation has not been fully investigated from the 'self' perspectives to date as most of the studies on the L2 Motivational Self System have focused on English learners. It is important to explore how learners' L2 self-images help enhance or decrease their motivation for learning Japanese. The purpose of the second question is to examine whether additional languages (both L1 and L2) influence and interact with the learners' commencement and engagement in the learning of Japanese and their future self-image as a Japanese user. As Henry (2017) claims, research into L2 motivation has had a so-called monolingual bias, and researchers have considered learner's motivational systems of different target languages separately, not holistically. Thus, answering to the second question will contribute to developing the neglected research area of motivation in multiple languages and uncovering the complex relationship between different languages within a learner. The third question aims to reveal dynamic patterns in the Japanese language learners' motivational changes. It will make an important contribution to the current debate within SLA, which increasingly emphasizes dynamic aspects of L2 motivation. The fourth question is important for understanding the way in which different sociocultural variables (including differences in academic context and individual's learning experience) impact on the L2 self and L2 motivation. By illuminating similarities and differences between the two contexts and between different individuals, this study will identify the context-specific developmental process of Japanese language learners' self-concepts and other motivational dispositions. In this book, the reader is confronted with the expanding scope of the development of L2 self and L2 motivation due to the longitudinal focus on and comparative analysis between different languages within a learner in different contexts. Insights gained through this study have significant implications for the conceptualization of L2 self in multilingual contexts, for understanding dynamics of motivation, as well as for ideal self-based pedagogical approach.

For definition, although there are numerous theoretical models encompassing different definitions of L2 motivation, this book employs one of the most widely accepted definitions proposed by Gardner (1985). That is, L2 motivation is comprised of three internal factors: *effort* (motivation), *desire to learn the language* (cognition) and *attitudes towards learning the language* (affect). As for the terms for different languages learners possess, L1, L2, L3 and so on are utilized throughout in this book to indicate the chronological order of acquisition. In other words, if a learner has learnt English when in high school before she/he started to learn Japanese at university, English and Japanese are treated as her/his L2 and L3, respectively, regardless of her/his competence. However, this usage is often problematic, especially within the framework of multilingualism. For instance, in the contexts of third language acquisition, two or more languages are often learned simultaneously and there is a greater diversity in the order of acquisition compared with second language acquisition (Jessner 2008a). In these contexts, chronological order of acquisition does not necessarily correspond to the dominance (breadth or frequency of use) of language. Moreover, in the contexts where two or more languages are spoken at home, it is often difficult to clarify the chronological order of acquisition. Taking all these considerations into account, in the present study, when a learner possesses two native languages, the languages are classified as L1 and L2 in order of each learner's perceived competence. Non-native-languages which the learner studied at school are then classified as her/his L3, L4, L5 and so on in the order in which she/he studied. Occasionally, the term L2 is also used to indicate all languages that they have learned or are learning in addition to their first language (L1), regardless of the order of acquisition.

Doing comparative research

Given the lack of studies examining Japanese learners' motivation in depth, as well as its relationship to identities and motivation relating to learning/using other languages, I considered a more exploratory, qualitative study is required. I also chose a qualitative approach to better capture the inherent complexity of learning motivation. In order to answer to the first research question, I decided to employ Dörnyei's (2005) L2 Motivational Self System and the concept of *domain of possible selves* (Unemori, Omoregie and Markus 2004) as the main conceptual frameworks. However, I also sought to remain open to unexpected variations in Japanese learners' motivation. For the purpose of addressing the second question, I considered it might be beneficial for the analysis to examine the relationship between different languages the learners possess by comparing the interplay between their L2 selves. As Huang, Hsu and Chen (2015: 37) argue, 'an accumulation of research addressing foreign language learning of multiple languages within diverse local contexts will provide insights into how cross-cultural factors affect the motivational properties of possible selves'. I decided to carry out two stages of face-to-face interviews separated by seven months with the aim of addressing the third question. A longitudinal study is suitable to capture the learners' motivational changes. In order to respond to the fourth question, I focused on two different Japanese as a foreign language (FL) contexts. I particularly considered that comparing both an English-speaking country, such as Australia, and a non-English-speaking country, such as Korea, would uncover various impacts of English on the learners' experience of learning Japanese.

Research contexts of this study

The present study involves university students who are studying in two different contexts: namely Australia and South Korea. These research contexts were chosen, in part, because I am familiar with and have knowledge about them. I taught in the Australian tertiary-level context and am therefore keen to understand the participants' motivation for learning Japanese in this setting. Prior to this, I also taught Japanese in a Korean university for several years. Thus, this sensitivity and the insider knowledge about these learning contexts may enable me to better explain or interpret certain aspects of the data during the analysis stages. In a more general sense, the two different contexts were chosen in order to enable a comparative perspective that can effectively reveal differences and similarities between how the contexts shape learners' experience. As many researchers (e.g. Dörnyei and Ushioda 2009; Sampasivam and Clément 2014) have argued, features of the context of acquisition seem to have quite profound implications for L2 learners' learning motivation. While both countries have a large number of university learners of Japanese in common (The Japan Foundation, 2017), they differ considerably in terms of their population, history, economy, religions and language, as well as the nature of their institutional and academic contexts.

Australian context

Australia is categorized as an English-speaking, Western country. While Australia is often characterized as a multicultural and multilingual country, having developed the first comprehensive *National Policy on Languages* (Lo Bianco, 1987) among English-speaking countries, it is also criticized as having 'a complacently monolingual mindset' (Clyne 2007: 12). Schmidt (2014) points out that Australians' reluctance to learn another language results not only from their attitude that 'the rest of the world speaks English anyway' but also from geographical isolation, questions of national identity and economic priorities. According to The Japan Foundation's (2017) latest survey, the overall number of Japanese learners in Australia in 2015 is 357,348, which represents the fourth largest learner population in the world. However, it is also reported that most learners of Australia are at beginner or intermediate levels and that just 6,420 (1.8 per cent) of Australian Japanese learners are university students. In addition, although Japanese is taught in most Australian universities, a large portion of students who begin Japanese learning in their first year of university do not continue with it in their second year (Learned Academics Special Projects [LASP] 2007, 2009; Northwood 2013).

Still, the university learners do have a high amount of linguistic diversity. The Australian Academy of the Humanities reported that 38 per cent of the university students speak a language other than English (LOTE) at home, with just under 50 per cent of the university Japanese beginner learners stating that they speak a variety of Chinese at home (LASP 2009: 12). At the university where the present study was conducted, nine languages, including Japanese, are taught. Japanese courses are classified into 'introductory', 'intermediate', 'proficient' and 'advanced' levels. The students in these levels include both students who are completing a major in Japanese studies and students from other disciplines who also take Japanese as their elective subject. There are also approximately 500 students who belong to the university's Japanese club, which organizes various social events focused on using Japanese or engaging with Japanese (popular) culture.

Korean context

Korea, however, is situated in East Asia and can be described as a relatively monolingual and homogeneous country. In recent years, the number of Japanese learners in Korea has been on a downward trend. Despite this, there are still over 556,000 learners, with Korea possessing the third largest Japanese learner population in the world (The Japan Foundation 2017). It is believed that the decline in learners is partly due to socioeconomic and political factors, such as China's economic rise, the negative images from the Great East Japan Earthquake and nuclear accidents and the deterioration of relations between Japan and Korea (The Japan Foundation 2017). Approximately 81 per cent of the learners are secondary school students, and, somewhat similar to Australia, a relatively small percentage (9.3 per cent) of students study Japanese at the tertiary level. In contrast to the Australian context, almost all the students' first language is Korean, although most have studied English as a compulsory subject at their schools.

The Korean university where the present research was carried out offers four language courses, namely English, Japanese, Chinese and German. There are four Japanese subjects: grammar, reading, composition and conversation. Each subject is further divided into 'elementary', 'intermediate' and 'advanced' levels. Most of the students in these Japanese classes belong to the Department of Japanology and take Japanese as a compulsory part of their major. The department is made up of around 100 students. The students take most of their subjects with other students in the same major. The department organizes assemblies of all students and staff, Japanese language performances, short exchange programs to a Japanese university for the winter holidays and a variety of social events such as excursions, sports events and dinners. Each teacher organizes an extracurricular study group to support their students' study of Japanese. Another noticeable point in this context is that two of the graduation requirements set by the department are 1) passing the second highest level (N2) of Japan-designed

---

[1] JLPT: a worldwide Japanese government-sponsored test to evaluate proficiency in Japanese of non-native speakers.
[2] JPT: a Japanese-language test organized by a Korean private enterprise, widely accepted in Korean universities.

Japanese-Language Proficiency Test (JLPT)[1] and 2) 600 (out of 990) marks in the Korean-designed Japanese Proficiency Test (JPT)[2]. Moreover, for the purpose of enhancing the students' qualifications for job hunting, the department officially encourages them to take the Test of English for International Communication (TOEIC) in addition to JLPT and JPT. Thus, it is easy to imagine that the students have to cope with substantial pressure in completing their graduation requirements and finding employment in their course of Japanese learning. In short, the Korean context shares both important similarities and differences to the Australian context. I felt that this could provide opportunities for interesting contrast or corroboration across cases and therefore help sharpen and enrich the current study's ability to contribute to our understandings of Japanese learners' motivation.

Participants

Twenty-six participants are involved in the present study. The first fourteen participants are students at an Australian university. All are enrolled in the intermediate or upper levels of Japanese. They are either first, second or third year students at the university, where degree programs are generally three to five years in duration. The second group of twelve are studying Japanese at a university in South Korea. They are also taking intermediate or upper level Japanese courses, and in their first, second or third year level at the university. Here, the completion of undergraduate degrees generally takes four years.

Data gathering and analysis

The elicitation of motivational data was conducted through two stages of face-to-face interviews, each separated by seven months. For the first round (Korea: November 2014, Australia: March 2015), the participants were asked about their family language(s), previous and current learning experiences of Japanese and (if relevant) other second languages, experiences of visiting (or intention/desire to visit) the countries where the languages they study are used and future plans associated with the languages they study. The interview (see Appendix 1) aimed to elicit an overall picture of their motivation for learning Japanese, as well as for additional languages. For the follow-up round (Korea: June 2015, Australia: October 2015), the interview questions (see Appendix 2) were designed to examine motivation as a dynamic phenomenon, investigate changes in their learning experience over the seven month period and shed light on the various factors which have caused any noted changes (or non-change) to their motivation. All interviews were conducted face-to-face with individual participants. Interviews in Australia were conducted either in English or Japanese, while interviews in Korea were carried out in either Korean or Japanese. Because of my inadequate command of Korean, I decided to employ interpreters for the Korean interviews. The interpreters were Japanese women who teach beginner-level Japanese at the university. They have taught some participants previously. However, they do not (and will not) teach the intermediate or upper levels which the participants may take during the period of the data collection. For the second interview with the Korean participants, Skype was utilized due to the geographical distance, and I employed an interpreter who is a Korean woman teaching Japanese at the Australian university.

The analysis aimed to identify common themes and patterns in the informants' motivational characteristics, and the approach was based on the procedures described by Richards (2003). While analyzing the dataset for the first Korean interview (November 2014), basic codes (e.g. *interest in Japanese language/culture, ideal Japanese self, ought-to English self, intention to study Japanese*) as well as categories/patterns (e.g. *I want to study Japanese forever, cooperative L2 selves*) were generated. These codes, categories and patterns were then reconsidered and revised while analyzing the data for the first Australian interview (March 2015). A similar process was applied to the analysis of the data from the second Korean (June 2015) and Australian (October 2015) interviews. Then, the categories/patterns emerged in the first studies, and those in the second studies were reorganized to establish broader patterns (e.g. *sustained motivational trajectory*).

The evidence of the participants' future L2 self-images were obtained particularly in their answers to the interview questions like: 'What are your goals of studying Japanese?', and 'When you think of your future career (or, relationship with your family members or friends, leisure activities), what languages do you think you might use?' As will be discussed in detail later, the difference between domain-specific goals/objects and the related self-guides is difficult to clarify. In this study, however, the informants' comments about their future goals were classified according to whether the answer was limited to a cognitive goal or seemed to incorporate a future self-image. For instance, when a Korean informant, Bosun, stated, 'I think my goal for studying Japanese is employment', his comment was interpreted showing his goal linked to the career domain as it does not seem to entail imagery. In contrast, when an Australian participant, Diane, said, 'I would really want to work in Japan, or work for trading company in Australia as a translator', her statement was considered to reflect her vision. That is, an image of her ideal Japanese self within the career domain of her future life.

Organization of the book

The book is made up of seven chapters. Chapter 1 outlines the background to the study and the rationale for its undertaking as well as the study aims and research questions. It also describes the approach and methods of research utilized in this study. Chapter 2 is divided into three parts. First, major L2 motivational research along with key motivational models and concepts, including Dörnyei's L2 Motivational Self System, is outlined. Since the concept of L2 self is considered to be a central component of L2 motivation, psychological literature concerning the concept of possible selves is reviewed. The final section outlines some perspectives in multilingualism research that are particularly important to investigate the motivational relationship between different languages within a learner. The first Korean study, detailed in Chapter 3, consists of the first round of data collection in Korea in November 2014. The first Australian study follows in Chapter 4, examining the first interview data obtained from the Australian participants in March 2015. Chapter 5, the second Korean study, and Chapter 6, the second Australian study, analyze the second-round interview data which was collected in June 2015 and October 2015, respectively. The results of the Korean and Australian studies are drawn together in Chapter 7, where they are compared and contrasted. In the chapter, conclusions, practical implications, limitations of the study and suggestions for future research are also presented. The reader is invited to consider: (1) important aspects of language learner's future self-guide, including the theoretical and practical implications of the concept of *domain of L2 self*, which have not drawn much attention to date, (2) differing effects of Global English as an L1 and as an L2 on the construction of multilingual vision and motivation to learn LOTEs and (3) dynamic patterns of motivation for learning Japanese identified in the two contexts, which are applicable to other LOTE learning contexts.

2

Understanding language learning motivation 'multilingually'

Perspectives on language learning motivation

Identification, integrativeness and L2 self

The study of language learning motivation has been an important research area in second language acquisition (SLA). Scholars have considered that motivation to learn a second language is qualitatively different from other types of learning motivation. This is partly because they believed that second languages are mediating factors between ethnolinguistic groups, and 'languages are typically learnt in the process of becoming a member of a particular group' (Gardner and Lambert 1972: 12). That is, unlike other school subjects, foreign language learners are expected to both acquire knowledge of a language and also to identify with the target language community and adopt its behaviour patterns. This argument was largely dependent on studies of first language (L1) acquisition. Previous theories of first language development in children posited that young children are motivated by a desire to be like their parents. Consequently, they imitate the language of parents, which leads to acquisition of the language. This tendency is called 'identification' (Mowrer 1950: 714). Although the concepts of identification and imitation share similarities, the former is more dynamic than the latter because 'identification carries the implication that the identifier not only acts like but also likes (and fears) the individual identified with' (Mowrer 1950: 715).

Gardner and Lambert (1959, 1972) believed that the concept of identification has relevance to the second language learning process since successful language learning takes place when a learner has strong interest in and desire to identify with another language group. However, the concept of identification in Mowrer's study of first language acquisition was not appropriate for explaining the process of second language learning. Identification in L1 acquisition is driven by reduction or satisfaction of basic biological needs of young children, while in most second language situations learners are driven by more social motives (Gardner and Lambert 1972). Gardner and Lambert therefore felt that identification was insufficient for explaining second language learners' motives and instead proposed the concept of *integrativeness*. Gardner (2001: 6) explained that 'the integratively motivated individual is one who is motivated to learn the second language, has a desire or willingness to identify with the other language community, and tends to evaluate the learning situation positively'.

From a conceptual point of view, however, the applicability of the concept of *integrativeness* to the learning of English in a globalized world was called into question. Gardner (2001: 5) describes integrativeness as reflecting 'a genuine interest in learning the second language in order to come closer to the other language community', which implies a psychological and emotional identification with the speakers of the target language. However, in the case of English, which has become a global *lingua franca*, it is difficult to explain learners' integrative motivation in terms of identification with a particular ethnolinguistic community. The recognition of this problem resulted in the reconsideration of the concept of integrativeness. While Gardner (2001) regarded integrativeness as involving emotional identification *with* another culture group, Dörnyei and Csizér (2002) instead conceived of it as an identification process *within* the individual's self-concept. This perspective led to an alternative motivational theory, the L2 Motivational Self System (Dörnyei 2005).

The L2 Motivational Self System

In recent personality psychology, the self is understood to be constantly changing and evolving, and each person is treated as possessing multiple selves (e.g. academic, physical and social). Possible Selves Theory (Markus and Nurius 1986) and Self-Discrepancy Theory (Higgins, Klein and Strauman 1985; Higgins 1987) represent this trend in explaining specific self-representations in relation to conceptualizations of future states. Both theories believe that images of oneself in the future function as incentives of behaviour and that people are motivated because of the desire to decrease the discomfort between one's current sense of self and their ideal or ought-to self. Under these conceptualizations, motivation is considered to be driven by a conscious striving to approach or avoid future selves (Higgins 1987).

Drawing on these psychological theories, Dörnyei (2005) proposed the L2 Motivational Self System, with the theory composed of the following three dimensions:

- *Ideal L2 self*, which involves the L2-specific aspect of one's ideal self. 'If the person we would like to become speaks an L2, the ideal L2 self is a powerful motivator to learn the L2 because of the desire to reduce the discrepancy between our actual and ideal selves' (Dörnyei 2005: 105).
- *Ought-to L2 self*, which represents the attributes that one believes one ought to possess and focuses on duties and obligations imposed by external authorities. If one feels pressured to learn an L2 in order to avoid an unfavourable end-state of not learning it, the ought-to self might be a strong driving force of learning. Although the ought-to self may bear little resemblance to the person's own wishes, there might be ideal cases when the ideal and the ought-to L2 selves coincide (Dörnyei 2014).
- *L2 Learning Experience*, which refers to the motivational impact of the immediate learning environment and experiences (e.g. the impact of the teacher, the peer group or the experience of success).

Since Gardner and Lambert's (1959) concept of integrative motivation, which indicated psychological and emotional 'identification' with the target language speakers, was inherited from Mowrer's (1950) concept of 'identification' with parents or caregivers in first language development, the focus of the concept was on external people or groups. Dörnyei's (2005) ideal L2 self, however, is related to individuals' 'identification' with their own future self-concepts. This shift in focus from external people to internal self-concepts made it possible to overcome the conceptual issues of integrative motivation that arose from issues like world English. That is, the self-perspective could explain the motivational setup within various learning contexts even if they provide learners with little or no contact with native speakers (Dörnyei and Csizer 2002).

One of the most significant advantages of the L2 Motivational Self System is that it can simultaneously address multiple motivations. As MacIntyre, MacKinnon and Clément (2009: 52) argue, '(m)otivation is multiply determined, with any single action involving a variety of competing motivational forces ... Language learning is integrated with all of the other activities in which a learner occupies his or her time'. The L2 Motivational Self System allows researchers to investigate various future selves and competing motives (e.g. L2 and L3 motivations) that learners experience (MacIntyre, MacKinnon and Clément 2009). Indeed, a number of studies which employed the theory have provided interesting findings about learners' motivation across multiple languages, which will be discussed later.

Motivation for learning Japanese

In the field of Japanese language education, a number of studies which examine learning motivation have been conducted in both foreign language acquisition (e.g. Nuibe, Kano and Ito 1995; Guo and Quan 2006; Nemoto 2011; Nishitani 2009; Matsumoto 2009; Northwood and Thomson 2012; Nakamura 2015, Djafri 2016) and SLA (e.g. Lee 2003; Harada 2010; Buasaengtham and Yoshinaga 2015) contexts. Most of these studies focus on students' motives to learn Japanese at a certain time and context by utilizing quantitative instruments. Although researchers started to emphasize the dynamics and temporal aspects of motivation (e.g. Nemoto 2011; Buasaengtham and Yoshinaga 2015), the intertwined relationship between learner's future self, motivation and environment has not been examined sufficiently.

When we look at Australia, one of the research contexts of the present study, Matsumoto (2009) investigated the motivational characteristics of 450 students who learn Japanese at three different universities. The results indicated that in Australian universities, learners' cultural/linguistic backgrounds (i.e. East Asian or Western) have a significant impact on their performance in learning Japanese and sustaining motivation. It was found that those learners who have distant cultural/linguistic backgrounds from Japanese tend to develop cultural interest, which positively influenced persistence in their study in turn. However, the closeness to Japanese language/culture often affects negatively East-Asian students' persistence because it may result in their development of an inappropriately high level of self-efficacy and lead to the discontinuity of their formal study of the language. Northwood and Thomson (2012) examined the factors that keep learners of Japanese going in formal study. By utilizing Gardner's (1985) SE model, the authors found that continuers showed much higher levels of motivation and integrative orientation. Also, the prominent reasons to continue with Japanese involved the hope to travel to Japan and an interest in Japanese culture and pop culture (J-pop). From the results of the follow-up interviews, the researchers suggested that learning Japanese is another way of consuming Japanese products (e.g. cosmetics, *manga* comics, drama series and J-pop songs), which means that students not only consume Japanese language but also consume Japanese language 'learning'. Based on these findings, Northwood (2013) further emphasized that *passion* for an activity may be an important factor which differentiates continuers and discontinuers. The author claimed that although the passion is considered to be the driving force in motivation, it may not always be connected to learning effort, as many students do not identify J-pop activities as 'learning' or 'effortful'. In order to investigate Australian Japanese language learners' motivations, Nakamura (2015) utilized the L2 Motivational Self System (Dörnyei, 2005) and the concept of *domain of possible selves* (Unemori, Omoregie and Markus 2004). The author focused not only on the formation of Japanese future self-image but also on the relationship between different L2 selves within a learner. While previous studies have emphasized negative impacts of an ideal English self-image on additional L2 selves, Nakamura's qualitative analysis of interview data from thirteen informants showed that the informants' ideal Japanese selves are often constructed in relation to their interest in Japanese pop culture. It also found that if one can clearly identify a future L2 self associated with at least one domain (i.e. interpersonal, extracurricular, career and education) of future life, multiple ideal L2 selves can coexist without any competition.

As for the other research context, Korea, there have been only a limited number of studies which examine Japanese language learning motivation. Lee (2003) compared motivation of 139 Japanese as second language (JSL) learners and that of 164 Japanese as foreign language (JFL) learners. Through comparing quantitative data, the author concluded that JFL learners are more likely to experience a difficulty in sustaining their motivation compared with JSL learners and that this tendency is due to the lack of Japan-related (i.e. visit, sojourn) experience and self-efficacy of the JFL learners. There is a growing recognition in the SLA field that self, motivation and sociohistorical context are inevitably related (Murray, Gao and Lamb 2011), and language learning motivation has been re-conceptualized and re-theorized in relation to self and identity (Dörnyei and Ushioda 2009). Thus, in order to deepen our understanding about Japanese learners' motivation, it is vital to incorporate the self-perspectives. The next section will, thus, examine how the concept of self in general, and possible self in particular, has been studied in psychological literature.

Possible selves

Self and self-concept

As has been mentioned above, while integrating a self-perspective in the area of language learning motivation is highly advantageous, one of the theoretical problems is how to define the constructions relating to 'self'. In psychology and sociology, there is no single definition of self, and many definitions refer to different phenomena (Leary and Tangney 2003). Moreover, 'different writers have used precisely the same terms differently, and sometimes individual writers have used "self" in more than one way within a single paper' (Leary and Tangney 2003: 6). In fact, even the two theories on which the L2 Motivational Self System is based, namely Markus and Nurius's (1986) possible selves theory and Higgins's (1987) self-discrepancy theory, have different perspectives in terms of the nature of an individual's self-concept.

Self-concept is considered to be the surface personality trait which is distinguished from the core personality traits represented by the Big Five personality factors, namely neuroticism, extraversion, conscientiousness, agreeableness, and openness. The core personality traits and multiple dimensions of self-concept exercise a reciprocal influence on each other, and both of them have important effects on human behaviour. However, unlike the core personality factors, which are not much affected by contextual factors, the self-concept is often influenced by contexts, environment and life events (Marsh et al. 2006). Oyserman and Fryberg (2006: 17) claim that 'self-concepts are what we think about when we think about ourselves. They are semantic, but also visual and affective representations of who we are, who we were, and who we can become'. Thus, self-concept is conceived of as a multifaceted structure containing a range of self-representations including past, current and future representations of self. However, not all the self-representations that consist of the self-concept are similar. Some self-concepts are more important and more elaborated than others. Some are more positive than others (Oyserman and Markus 1990: 113).

Although the term *identity* is often used in a similar manner with self-concept, studies investigating either construct generally have a distinct emphasis and focus. Mercer (2011) says that self-concept represents a core or an inner psychological sense of self, which individuals take with them into different contexts, whereas the concept of identity is used when the emphasis is more on the social nature of the self and a person's relationship with others. Thus, identity is 'constructed on the base of an individual's self-concept but is concerned primarily with the relationship between the individual's sense of self and a particular social context or community of practice' (Mercer 2011: 19).

Possible selves and future self-guides

While conventional research on the functioning of the self-concept mainly focused on features of the self relating to one's past and present behaviours,

Markus and Nurius (1986) shed light on future or *possible selves*. According to the authors, possible selves have cognitive components of hopes, fears, goals and threats, made up of three distinct parts: the *expected self*, the *hoped-for self* and the *feared self*. The expected self is a future self that a person feels one can realistically achieve, and it may be positive or negative in nature. The hoped-for self is a highly desired possible self. Examples might include the successful self, the rich self or the loved and admired self. The feared self is instead what a person is afraid of becoming, such as the incompetent self, the unemployed self or the alone self. Possible selves are important because they function as incentives for future behaviour and also provide an evaluative context for the current view of self (Markus and Nurius 1986). An important aspect which distinguishes possible selves theory from other psychological theories is that it involves imagery components as motivational constructs. Markus and Nurius (1986) argue that the imagery of the self in a future state is perceived similarly to the way in which the current self is perceived. That is to say, the created future image is experiential for the individual and thus could function as a powerful motivator.

Having argued for the significance of self-relevant imagery in human motivation, how does it serve as a powerful motivator? The Self-Discrepancy Theory (Higgins 1987) provides a reasonable explanation for this process. Prior to Markus and Nurius's (1986) work, Tory Higgins and his associates (Higgins, Klein and Strauman 1985) suggested that there are two types of idealized future selves that have impact on behaviour: the *ideal self* and *ought self*. In this theory, motivation involves the desire to reduce the discrepancy between one's *actual self* (self-concept) and the ideal/ought selves (future self-guides). According to Higgins (1987), sufficient discrepancy between one's current sense of self and his/her future self-guides causes discomfort which, in turn, leads to various motivational behaviours aimed at reducing the discomfort. Although the theory has a potential to cause confusion since the ideal and ought selves are similar to each other in that they are related to a desired future-state, the author explained that the difference between these future-oriented selves is reflected in the traditional conflict between one's 'personal wishes' and 'sense of duty' (Higgins 1987: 321). That is, the ideal self-guides involve a *promotion* focus, whereas ought-to self-guides have a *prevention* focus (Crowe and Higgins 1997). To sum up, Markus and Nurius's theory emphasizes the role of imagery components in the generation of motivation, whereas Higgins's theory focuses more on the role of cognition (i.e. one's recognition of a discrepancy between the individual's current and future selves).

In addition to this aspect, there is another important conceptual difference between the two theories in terms of the nature of future selves. On the one hand, Markus and Nurius take the perspective that the individual possesses a diversity of domain-specific possible selves. As we can see in the literature of possible selves (e.g. Markus and Nurius 1986; Oyserman and Markus 1990; Oyserman, Bybee and Terry 2006), various domains of possible selves (e.g. academic, health-related) have been investigated to date. It is assumed that not all the possible selves work concurrently. Rather, they are differentially accessible, and particular domain-specific selves are activated at particular times and contexts (Oyserman, Bybee and Terry 2006). From this point of view, a language learner who uses or is learning plural languages may have distinct future self-images for each language. On the other hand, Higgins views the self as a unitary construct possessing a variety of facets. In other words, the plural language learner has a single ideal self and single ought self, and each future self-guide includes L2 and L3 dimensions (see also Henry 2011). This conceptual difference is important to the current study, which investigates motivational relationship between different languages within individuals. Accordingly, it will be discussed further in the following section.

Possible selves as social constructions

The construction of possible selves has been one of the main interests of research of possible selves. As Oyserman, Bybee and Terry (2006) point out, possible selves can be rooted in an individuals' past experiences or accomplishments. For example, students who have attained a high grade may find it easier to imagine positive academic possible selves than those who have not. Possible selves can also stem from what significant others believe one should become. For some students, the ideals their parents hold for them can be the root of their self-representation. For others, peer groups can act as reference groups which influence the construction of self-guides. Other potential sources of possible selves include one's own values, ideas and aspirations and the influence of role models (Dörnyei 2009). Thus, possible selves appear to be the result of various factors. However, many scholars (e.g. Markus and Nurius 1986; Quinlan, Jaccard and Blanton 2006; Oyserman and Fryberg 2006) agree that one of the most fundamental characteristics of possible selves is that they are 'importantly social' (Oyserman and Fryberg 2006). Even when possible selves appear to be individualized and personalized, they are the result of previous social comparisons of oneself and salient others. As Markus and Nurius (1986: 954) stress, 'the pool of possible selves derives from the categories made salient by the individual's particular sociocultural and historical context and from the models, images, and symbols provided by the media and by the individual's immediate social experiences'. Possible selves are not independently owned and controlled but socially conditioned and constructed. Therefore, when examining language learners' L2 self, it is necessary to understand how their language-specific visions are constructed within particular sociocultural, historical and linguistic contexts.

Generation, achievement and elimination of possible selves

The role of possible selves in the initiation, maintenance and cessation of human behaviour has also been a central research interest, since possible selves have been regarded as the self-system that moves people to action and are thus fundamental for motivation (Markus and Ruvolo 1989). Dunkel and his colleagues (2006) argue that in a therapeutic setting successful and sustained behavioural change, which involves a change in the possible selves, occurs in the following five stages. In the first stage, individuals are either unaware of having a personal problem that needs changing or are aware of the problem but refuse to change, and therefore, the number of possible selves is limited. In the second stage, an individual is aware of the problem, and thus thinking about change. At this stage, individuals generate a greater number of possible selves since they are engaged in self-exploration. The next stage is when individuals have decided to change and are preparing for action. It is predicted that the decision to pursue some possible selves will lead to the elimination of other possible selves. Thus, the total number of their possible selves should decrease. In the fourth stage, individuals make an effort to change their own problematic behaviour. As the commitment to their chosen possible selves continues, the elimination of contradictory possible selves will also continue. In the final stage, individuals' behaviours have been changed and the problem has been mitigated or resolved. As the chosen possible selves are integrated in one's current self-concept, they are no longer seen as future possibility. That is, 'once the possible self is validated it is eliminated from the range of possibilities and incorporated into the repertoire of current selves' (Dunkel, Kelts and Coon 2006: 189). In addition, possible selves concerning a domain, in which the self has been attained, may still be produced or updated. This argument is particularly useful when exploring dynamic relationships between language learners' L2 self and their learning behaviour.

Feared self

Importantly, merely having a possible self-image does not necessarily provide motivation or affect behaviour, and some possible selves are more likely to influence current behaviour than others. This means that there are conditions under which possible selves can have an impact on people's behaviour. One of the conditions is that a possible self will be a most effective motivator when it is offset or balanced by a countervailing self in the same domain (Oyserman and Markus 1990). That is, a positive expected self will be a powerful motivational resource when it is connected with a feared self-image of what could happen if the desired end state is not attained (e.g. a youth's self-representations of 'high school graduate' and 'high school dropout'). Moreover, when possible selves are balanced, people use strategies that both increase the possibility of achieving the desired future self and decrease the possibility of attaining the unwanted future self, thus facilitating self-regulation (Oyserman, Bybee and Terry 2006). Hoyle and Sherrill (2006) also suggest that off-setting or balanced possible selves provide stronger motivation than single future self-image alone. The researchers explain, 'the motivation conferred by balanced possible selves is additive and therefore greater than the motivation conferred by the hoped-for or feared possible self alone. Additionally, balanced possible selves tap both approach and avoidance motives, thereby broadening the repertoire of behaviours relevant for the desired outcome' (Hoyle and Sherrill 2006: 1677). This point of view is important for investigating language learning motivation because some language learners are likely to imagine not only their ideal L2 selves but also their feared self-images in which they lose proficiency in the target language.

This section sought to summarize some of the main findings in possible selves research and its implication for language learning motivation. However, while psychological literature has produced valuable contributions, it has not provided a contextualized understanding of self-concept or offered insights into the complexity and uniqueness of individual learners or contexts (Mercer 2011: 3). Thus, in order to illuminate how the future representation develops and interacts with dynamic contexts, a form of inquiry that retains a holistic view of L2 learners is required.

Multilingual perspectives

While the multiplicity of learners' self and identity has been emphasized in L2 motivation research to date (e.g. Ushioda 2009), and many students use or learn more than one foreign language (Cenoz, Hufeisen and Jessner 2001; LASP 2007), the possible motivational factor of learners' L2 self in additional languages has been largely neglected. Taking a multilingualist perspective, Herdina and Jessner (2002) argue that looking at the languages in terms of isolated development may not make sense because the behaviour of each individual language in a multilingual user largely depends on the behaviour of previous and subsequent languages. Therefore, to investigate Japanese learners' L2 selves and their motivational impacts, we need to take a more holistic view which includes not only Japanese but also all languages the individuals possess.

The Dynamic Model of Multilingualism (DMM)

A comprehensive explanation about the relationship among different languages within multilingual individuals was offered by Philip Herdina and Ulrike Jessner (2002). The researchers emphasized that languages within individuals change and continuously interact with each other and are influenced by various internal/external factors. Drawing on SLA theory, bilingual research and dynamic systems theory (DST), the researchers proposed the Dynamic Model of Multilingualism (DMM), which has the following main characteristics (Herdina and Jessner 2002; Jessner 2008b):

- The model considers languages in individuals as dynamic systems forming part of a psycholinguistic system, because these language systems are characterized by continuous change and non-linear growth.
- Psycholinguistic systems are defined as open systems depending on psychological and social factors.
- Language choice or use (i.e. who will speak which language, when and to whom) depends on the perceived communicative needs of the multilingual speaker.
- Systems stability is related to language maintenance; that is, the system will erode if not enough energy and time is invested in maintaining the system.
- Language systems are seen as interdependent rather than autonomous systems.
- The holistic approach is a necessary prerequisite for understanding the dynamic interaction between complex systems in multilingualism.

This model, which first employed DST on multilingualism, provided a sound basis for the current debate on language learning motivation that L2 and L3 motivations within a learner are dynamic systems, which are constantly interacting with each other (cf. Ushioda 2017; Henry 2017). Another important theoretical contribution of the DMM is that it conceives of the gradual language loss as a function of language acquisition. The model explains that multilingual speakers (of any level) have a certain amount of time and energy available to spend on language learning and maintenance. Accordingly, if not enough time and energy is spent on refreshing the knowledge of an L2, the learner will gradually lose the L2 because of the natural principle of entropy. For instance, in a monolingual society, an individual speaker in isolation has an intrinsic tendency towards monolingualism, since monolingualism is the natural state of a speaker (Herdina and Jessner 2002). The DMM also suggests that language loss or decay is counteracted by use of the language and that the stability of a language system is dependent on the requirements of language maintenance effort, although other possible factors (e.g. the number of languages involved, maturational age at which a language is learnt, the level of proficiency) may also contribute to the stability (Jessner 2008b). Here, one of the most important factors which may help the language maintenance effort is called *domain specificity*.

Domain of language behaviour

Domain of language behaviour refers to 'a sphere of activity representing a combination of specific times, settings and role relationships' (Romaine 1989: 29). In each domain of life, there may be 'pressures of various kinds, including economic, administrative, cultural, political, and religious, which influence the bilingual towards use of one language rather than the other' (Romaine 1989: 30). Herdina and Jessner (2002: 105) also claim as follows:

> As, however, languages rarely cover all domains of life equally and speech communities are seldom that homogeneous, we are likely to come across a multilingual phenomenon called domain specificity [see Downes, 1984: 49; Fishman, 1972], which will probably give rise to a functional differentiation within the multilingual language system which may be topic-specific, situation-specific or group-specific (see Gumperz, 1972; Romaine, 1989: 151). The introduction of domain specificity will of course contribute to the stabilisation of the multilingual language system as the languages are no longer functionally equivalent and interchangeable but fulfil a complementary role in the daily communicative requirements of the multilingual individual in her/his society.

This functional differentiation, which leads to the creation of a stable system, 'not only has a drastic effect on the amount of maintenance required for a specific language system but also reduces the risk of interference to a minimum'

(Herdina and Jessner 2002: 105). Moreover, the concept of domain specificity may also be useful to understand the relationship between different language-specific visions, since the studies of possible selves (e.g. Oyserman and James 2009; Oyserman et al. 2004) have considered that future self-images may develop in domains relevant to current life domains (e.g. academic, occupational).

The importance of domain specificity in researching bi/multilinguals was emphasized from a different perspective by Grosjean (2008, 2010), who proposed the *complementarity principle* of bilingualism. According to the author (Grosjean 2008: 23), '(b)ilinguals usually acquire and use their languages for different purposes, in different domains of life, with different people. Different aspects of life often require different languages'. All bilinguals have differing language-use patterns covering domains such as parents, children, siblings, work, sports, religion, school, shopping, hobbies, and so on. Some languages will spread over many domains, whereas others will cover fewer domains. Some languages will be used exclusively in particular domains, while the other will be used in particular domains with another language or other languages (Grosjean 2010). Also, if a language is spoken in a limited number of domains and with a limited number of people, then the fluency of the language will be less developed than a language used in more domains and with more people (Grosjean 2010).

While the concept of domain-specificity has been primarily concerned with bi/multilinguals' language acquisition and use in context, SLA research to date has not paid much attention to the concept's theoretical importance. One exception is Mercer (2011), who utilized the concept of domain-specificity in a study investigating university language learners' multiple self-concepts. In her view, the learners' domain involves various spheres of university life, such as academic, math, physical, foreign language, English and Italian (see also Mills 2014: 10; Rubio 2014: 43). However, since L2 self-concept is classified as one of the academic self-concepts (e.g. geography, history), it is relatively isolated from the various life domains outside of the university. In this sense, adapting the complementary principle may have benefits for the analysis of the language learners' future L2 self-concept and motivation, as it takes account of the whole contexts, not just the university, in which language learners will later acquire or use the target language (cf. Lyons 2014).

Bi/multilingual identities

It seems that there are two contrasting views on the self-concepts connected to different languages within a person. On the one hand, there is a perspective that different linguistic and cultural self-concepts are stored separately within bilingual individuals (e.g. Herdina and Jessner 2002; Jessner 2008b; Cross and Gore 2003; Marsh, Byrne and Shavelson 1988; Mercer 2011; Pavlenko 2006). On the other hand, some researchers in bilingualism (e.g. Block 2006; Kanno 2003; Grosjean 2008) believe that two different languages (and cultures) within a bilingual are not separated but form a single or 'hybrid' self-concept. The former supposes that bi- and multilinguals may perceive the world differently and change ways of thinking and/or verbal and non-verbal behaviours when switching languages. From the results of a questionnaire survey which targeted 1,039 college students in the UK, Pavlenko (2006) found that a bilingual's duality or multiplicity of identities may emerge through the use of different languages linked to differing cultures. Mercer (2011) also claimed that there is a distinct self-concept for each language and proposed a number of internal (e.g. internal comparisons across domains and/or belief systems) and external (e.g. social comparison processes, feedback and reflected appraisals) factors that seemed to contribute to the development of a learner's foreign language self-concept.

In contrast to these views, Grosjean (2008, 2010) sees that the bilingual is not the sum of two monolinguals. Defining bilinguals as 'those people who use two or more languages (or dialects) in their everyday lives' (Grosjean 2008: 10), the author insists that the bilingual person has a unique and special linguistic system and therefore cannot easily be decomposed into two separate components. While there has been a long-standing argument that bilinguals have double or split personalities and unconsciously change their personality when they switch languages, his holistic view of bilingualism suggests that 'what is seen as a change in personality is simply a shift in attitudes and behaviours corresponding to a shift in situation or context, independent of language' (Grosjean 2010: 125). This point of view corresponds to Block's (2006) perspective that bilinguals do not add a new self-concept to an old one but rather create a mixed, *hybrid* identity. The concept of *bilingual identities* offered by Kanno (2003) also criticizes the 'two monolinguals within a person' perspective.

Bi/multilingual motivation

Ushioda (1998) emphasized that motivation for learning a second language should be considered in relation to motivation for other subjects, yet it is not an easy task to research multiple motivations that language learners possess. While scholars working in the multilingual paradigm in relation to phonology, morphology, syntax and pragmatics have all demonstrated the positive effects of cross-linguistic influence of L2 on the acquisition of subsequent languages, the effect of cognitive/affective factors on the third language (L3) acquisition process remains a largely uncharted area (Henry 2012). Nonetheless, a few studies have focused on the motivation related to learning several target languages within the same community (Csizér and Dörnyei 2005; Henry 2010, 2011; Dörnyei and Chan 2013; Dörnyei and Clément 2001; Csizér and Lukács 2010; Zaragoza 2011; Huang, Hsu and Chen 2015). Most of these studies are quantitative and suggest that the L2 and L3 are closely related to each other in terms of learning motivation. Interestingly, these studies consistently found that when the L2 is English, it has a negative influence on one's L3 learning motivation.

While recognizing benefits of learning more than one foreign language, Csizér and Dörnyei (2005) point out the negative influences of the L2 on the L3. The authors claim that 'being motivated to learn more than one L2 at the same time also causes interferences in that positive attitudes toward one language can exist at the expense of another. Thus, there is a "competition" among target languages for learners' limited language learning capacity, and in this competition the clear winner appears to be World English' (Csizér and Dörnyei (2005: 657). Dörnyei and Chan (2013) sought to reveal the presence of independent L2 selves. The result of a questionnaire survey from 172 Chinese secondary students who study English and Mandarin indicated that the development of an individual's L2 self is largely dependent on the learner's capability to generate mental imagery. The study further showed that the ideal L2 self-images associated with different target languages are distinct, thus constructing different L2-specific visions.

In order to explore the impact of L2 (English) on four Swedish secondary students' ideal/ought-to L3 selves, Henry (2011) adapted the framework of *working self-concept* (Markus and Nurius 1986: 957), which refers to the 'set of self-conceptions that are presently accessible in thought and memory'. The results obtained from in-depth analysis of the interview data indicate that while L2 English self-concept has a negative impact on L3 motivation in a school setting, some students were able to reduce such effects by recruiting a positive self-concept into the working self-concept. For example, when one of the participants had to read a difficult text in the Russian classroom, he often had a desire to read it in English instead of Russian. In other words, the English-speaking/using self-concept formed a dominant presence in the working self-concept and had a forceful impact on his Russian-speaking/using self-concept. However, he was able to overcome this problem by recruiting and activating 'a different view of self as being indomitable, focused and persevering' into his working self-concept (Henry 2011: 247).

Henry (2014: 8) also focused on the concept of 'competition' between different L2 selves. In his view, when the L2 is English, the competition of L2 selves is more likely to be experienced. Since English is often the first foreign language people learn in school, being increasingly present in the surrounding social environment, 'there is a risk that a dominant L2 English-speaking/using self-concept may gradually erode the vitality of an L3 language-speaking/using self-concept less central to the learner's overall identity' (Henry 2014: 8). This means that the ideal L2 self in an additional language will be negatively affected by the competing ideal English self-image (see also Csizér and Lukács 2010). Indeed, it has been argued elsewhere (Oyserman 2007) that when one has multiple goals in a particular domain, not all goals can be pursued simultaneously, or pursued with equal energy.

To sum up, the studies above show that in situations of multiple learning, individuals' different second languages may form different language specific visions and that these self-concepts have an effect on each other. In addition, when the L2 is English, one's learning motivation in an additional language tends to be negatively affected. However, the qualitative nature of different language-specific self-views and the relationship between them remains largely unknown, since most of these studies have adopted a quantitative research approach (Zaragoza 2011). Even in Henry's (2012) study, which utilized a qualitative approach to investigate learners' different L2 selves, the focus is on the learner's current or working self-concept at the micro level. The temporal flow or developmental process of L2 self has not been fully explored. As Csizér and Lukács (2010) emphasize, longitudinal studies which focus on the macro social context and on how the interplay of two or more foreign languages influences learners' motivational characteristics might be required. Recently, in the special issue of *The Modern Language Journal* entitled 'Beyond Global English: Motivation to Learn Languages in a Multicultural World', Ushioda and Dörnyei (2017) called for more research into language learning motivation from a multilingual perspective. Further, two studies (Ushioda 2017; Henry 2017) in the same issue claimed that L2 motivation research will benefit from investigating learners' multilingual vision or *ideal multilingual self*. The present study, which explores longitudinal development of Japanese language learners' bi/multilingual vision, will thus significantly contribute to the current debate on language learning motivation.

Conceptual frameworks

The overall purpose of the present study is to examine the motivational development of Japanese language learners, focusing on the development of their future Japanese self-images and their broader self-images as bilingual or multilingual individuals. To do this, I utilize Gardner's (1985) conventional definition of L2 motivation, which comprises three internal factors: *effort* (motivation), *desire to learn the language* (cognition) and *attitudes towards learning the language* (affect). Additionally, I employ Dörnyei's (2005) L2 Motivational Self System as a conceptual framework, since it addresses multiple motivations. While Dörnyei's (2005) L2 Motivational Self System brought about a theoretical shift in motivational orientation (i.e. from an external group to internal self-image), the traditional definition of L2 motivation has not been altered by the theory, which is why I adopt it as-is. According to Dörnyei and Ushioda (2011: 86), the three components of the L2 Motivational Self System (the ideal L2 self, the ought-to L2 self, and L2 learning experience) are the 'primary sources of the motivation to learn a second/foreign language'.

In addition to the L2 Motivational Self System, I also employ the concept of the *domain of possible selves* (Oyserman and Markus 1990; Unemori, Omoregie and Markus 2004). Since an ideal L2 self is 'the L2-specific facet of one's ideal self' (Dörnyei 2005: 105), it is likely that one's L2/L3 self-images can similarly be categorized into certain domains. Although the developmental process of language learners' L2 self in particular social environments has been investigated (e.g. Kim 2009; Lamb 2009), little attention has been devoted to the content of their future self-images. In general motivational psychology, for example, Oyserman and James (2009: 373) claimed that 'individuals possess multiple positive and negative possible selves. These possible selves are often linked with differing social roles and identities, so that possible selves are likely to develop in domains relevant to current life tasks such as being a student, a parent or a life partner'. For a better understanding of learners' L2 self, it therefore might be necessary to investigate the domains in which their L2 self-image is constructed. In my previous study (Nakamura 2015), which investigated Australian Japanese language learners' future L2 self-images, I employed Unemori, Omoregie and Markus's (2004: 326) thematic categories of possible selves (*intrapersonal, interpersonal, career/education, extracurricular, attainment of material goods* and *health related*). Through the analysis of the data, the original schema was modified, and the following four domains of future life were extracted:

1. Interpersonal domain (communicating with friends, communicating with family, mediator)
2. Extracurricular domain (enjoying media, enjoying other hobbies)
3. Career domain (desired job)
4. Education domain (study abroad plan, concern for grades, mastering the language)

This categorization system is adopted as the basis for an analytical framework in the current study. Since these domains were derived from the Australian university context, where students possess a variety of cultural backgrounds, I considered that they might also be applicable to university students in different cultural contexts.

Lastly, as one of the purposes of the current study is to depict the dynamism of Japanese language leaners' motivation, I also utilize DST (e.g. Larsen-Freeman and Cameron 2008; Van Geert 2008; Dörnyei, MacIntyre and Henry 2015), especially for the data analysis of the second interview. As Dörnyei and his colleagues (Dörnyei, MacIntyre and Henry 2015: 5) point out, L2 motivation and L2 self-guide are 'by nature inherently dynamic and would therefore be well suited targets for investigation using dynamic approaches'. In the present study, which investigates the developmental process of L2 learners' motivation, DST is considered to be particularly beneficial to understand how motivational fluctuations were triggered and how the changes of motivational constructs occur. In DST, the L2 learners' motivation is conceptualized as a dynamic system, and the system is considered to be in constant interaction with other systems and the contexts in which it is embedded (Henry 2017). De Bot, Lowie and Verspoor (2007: 14) explained that a language learner is 'a dynamic subsystem within a social system with a greater number of interacting internal dynamic sub-sub-systems … The learner has his/her own cognitive ecosystem consisting of intentionality, cognition, intelligence, motivation, aptitude, L1, L2 and so on'.

In line with the perspectives of DST and the L2 Motivational Self System, the present study conceptualizes Japanese learners' motivation as a *Japanese motivational system*, which is composed of three main subsystems: (1) the ideal Japanese self, (2) the ought-to Japanese self, and (3) Japanese learning experience. However, I remain open to the possibility of identifying other motivational concepts as the subsystems. This is because the L2 Motivational Self System was developed primarily in the contexts of study of English, and its applicability to the motivational systems of languages other than English is still unknown (Dörnyei 2005; Ushioda and Dörnyei 2017).

3

'Japanese is easy but difficult to continue.' Motivation and future self-images of Korean learners

The objective in Chapters 3 and 4 is to provide participants' accounts of their motivations for initially starting and then continuing with their study of Japanese at school and university, as well as a snapshot of the participants' L2 self, L2 learning experience and current motivation at the time of the initial interview (i.e. for most students within the first year or two of their university study). For this chapter, I will first examine the Korean participants' L2 learning experiences when in high school and university. Within the framework of the L2 Motivational Self System, the concept of *L2 learning experience* has been most commonly used in relation to the motivational impact of 'the immediate learning environment and experience (e.g. the impact of teacher, the curriculum, the peer group, the experience of success)' (Dörnyei 2009: 29). However, little attention has been paid to L2 *use* experience outside of the classroom. Since the data indicates that both L2 learning and L2 use experiences can have a considerable impact on motivation, the current study refers to both L2 learning and use experiences as *L2 learning experience*.

Background of the Korean participants

Twelve students (two female and ten male) participated in the interviews conducted at a Korean university in November 2014. For the first interview, eight of the interviews were conducted in Korean through an interpreter, while four participants chose to have the interview conducted in Japanese. In this section, the participants' quotes from the interviews conducted in Japanese are shown in both Japanese and in English translation, while those from the interviews carried out in Korean are displayed only in English. Since I have limited knowledge of Korean language, I asked a Korean–English bilingual speaker to double-check the English translation of some interview extracts. All participants had learnt English as a compulsory school subject and Japanese at junior high or high school for periods ranging from a few months to five years. Three of them had also learnt Russian, German or Mandarin. However, since they had studied these languages for relatively short periods of time and also did not have any related sojourn experiences, they appeared to have little impact on their study of Japanese and English. Thus, the focus of analysis mainly considered their motivation for learning Japanese and English, as well as the motivational relationship between them. The background of the participants is presented in Table 3.1. **Bold** type represents those languages they were studying at the university at the time of the interview. All the four participants who have learnt L4 did not have any sojourn experience to the countries where the languages are spoken.

Learning experience of Japanese

Interest in Japanese pop culture

The interview data showed a number of trends in the Korean participants' study of Japanese at high school. First of all, their interest in Japanese culture played a significant role in stimulating their study of the language. Five of the participants said that their initial reason for starting Japanese language learning was because of their personal interest in Japanese pop culture, such as animation, TV programmes and video games. Interestingly, their current interests are sometimes connected to their vision of a future state. Cheonga, for example, commented, 'I found it interesting and fun to watch Japanese TV dramas and entertainment shows. I thought that if I study Japanese, then, I would be able to watch these shows without subtitles'.

From a perspective of the L2 self, Cheonga might imagine a clear future self as a Japanese user who is enjoying Japanese TV programmes. This future self-concept is specifically formulated in relation to her current hobbies and constructed personally. In many cases, the Korean informants' self-images as a Japanese user derived from their interests in the pop culture were not linked to the distant future. Nonetheless, a few informants' current interests in the language/culture appeared to evolve in relation to their future goals or self-images. Especially for

Table 3.1 Background of Korean participants

Name (pseudonym)	Age	Year level	L2/formal study	Sojourn experience	L3/formal study	Sojourn experience	L4/formal study
1 Anbok	19	1	English 9 years	1 month (New Zealand)	Japanese 1 year		
2 Junha	20	1	**English 13 years**		Japanese 6 years	10 days 20 days	
3 Oyeon	20	1	**English 11 years**		Japanese 4 years	4 days 1 week	**Mandarin** 3 months
4 Ihyeong	22	2	English 10 years		Japanese 6 years		
5 Minseop	22	2	English 10 years		Japanese 4 years	2 weeks	Russian 3 months
6 Bosun	22	2	English 6 years		Japanese 5 years		
7 Nampyo	23	2	English 11 years		Japanese 3 years		German 2 years
8 Cheonga	20	2	English 11 years		Japanese 4 years	5 days 5 days	
9 Daebeon	23	3	English 10 years		Japanese 4 years	5 days	
10 Gapsang	23	3	English 12 years		Japanese 4 years	1 week	
11 Hongdae	26	3	English 10 years		Japanese 5 years	1 week	
12 Pilho	26	4	English 10 years		Japanese 11 years	1 week 1 year	German 6 months

those who did not have a clear future goal, one's current interest or enjoyment in Japanese-related activities/hobbies (e.g. animation, video games) helped one's exploration of possible selves in the distant future.

For instance, when Ihyeong was a high school student, he often played Japanese video games. Although he was unsure about his course after graduation, the hobby helped him envision a future self-image of learning Japanese in university. The following quote illustrates how his interest contributed to the decision to study Japanese:

> Because I really liked Sony's Play Station, I learned Japanese naturally through playing games, or things like that. I had not studied the language intensely until the third year of high school … At the time of university entrance exam, when the questions of what I am able to do and what I am interested in troubled me, I decided to study Japanese at university because I thought I might be good at the language.

Ihyeong's sense of self as a gamer, which is created through his favourite hobby related to Japanese, might help him envision an ideal Japanese self in the distant future. Possession of an interest in Japanese culture, such as pop songs and video games, can be a potential source for an initial sense of oneself as a Japanese user and for formulating one's long-term Japanese self-image.

Self-study

Second, the Korean informants in general preferred to study Japanese not at school, but by themselves. All informants had studied Japanese at either their junior high or high school. While six of them took Japanese as a compulsory subject for periods ranging from one semester to three years, the others chose it as an elective foreign language. Interestingly, hardly any informant reported that they enjoyed the study of Japanese in the classroom. Rather, those informants who were interested in the language tended to study it by themselves as a personal hobby. Pilho reported as follows:

> 大学入学テストのための勉強しかやらないじゃないですか、高校の授業は。日本語というのは自分がやりたくて始めたので。… 半分趣味で勉強してました。… 基本的に教科書を買って、ずっと一人で勉強して、単語を暗記して、それと同時に日本のアニメを主に見てました。で、たぶん高校卒業の頃は日本語の原書を読みながら、それを翻訳してみたり、歌を聴きながら韓国語に翻訳してみたりしました。

[In high school classes, we study only for the university entrance exam. But, I kind of studied Japanese … as a hobby, because it was what I wanted to study … I bought a text book, taught myself it, and memorized the vocabulary. At the same time, I primarily watched Japanese *anime*. Then, at the time of the graduation, I read Japanese books and listened to Japanese songs, and tried translating them into Korean.]

While Pilho reported that he was not fond of studying English as a compulsory subject for the university entrance exams, the study of Japanese was perceived as a 'hobby'. Similarly, two other participants (Anbok and Oyeon) also commented that they taught themselves Japanese apart from their study in high school, since the difficulty level of Japanese taught in high school was not satisfactory to them. This may reflect the lack of relevance of classroom practices at school to their personal interests.

Japanese as a short-term goal

This trend toward self-study appears to be linked to the participants' perceived ease of learning Japanese. As Junha, Anbok, Minseop and Pilho described Japanese as an 'easy' language, all four may believe that certain levels of proficiency in Japanese can be achieved in a relatively short period of time. For instance, Junha reported as follows:

> （日本の）アニメを見る時は、韓国語の字幕をつけて一緒に見る。そうやったら、韓国語と日本語は語順が同じですね。すごい、（アニメでは韓国語と日本語が）一緒に出ますから、それを自然に習うことができました。

[When watching Japanese *anime*, I add Korean subtitles. Korean and Japanese have the same word order, don't they? That's great. I was able to learn Japanese naturally, because Korean and Japanese appear simultaneously on the *anime*.]

Two participants (Anbok and Oyeon) said that they studied Japanese in order to obtain academic credentials. For example, Anbok studied hard to get the highest certificate of JLPT (N1). The quote below best describes how he was motivated to get the credential:

I: 高校の授業とは別にＮ１の本をずっと勉強をしていた？
S: はい、学校のほうはほったらかして。
I: 高校のときはあまり（日本のアニメ・マンガを）見なかったの？

S: はい、ただＮ１をとる（ことだけで）、ほかの事は目に入らなくて。
I: その当時、日本語を将来使うと思っていましたか？
S: 日本語は、たしかに使うと思います。でも中国語とか英語よりは（使う機会は）少ないと（思いました）。

[I: So, did you study N1 books apart from Japanese class in high school?
S: Yes. Even neglecting school study.
I: And so, you didn't watch Japanese *anime* or *manga* when in high school?
S: No. I focused on taking N1 and ignored other things.
I: At that time, did you think you would use Japanese in the future?
S: I thought I would use Japanese. But, I also thought that there would be less opportunities to use the language, compared with Mandarin and English.]

Anbok seemed to envision a clear future self-representation, in which he attains the N1, but this clear goal might overshadow all other potential interests (e.g. Japanese pop culture) or goals. In the extract presented above, he considered Japanese to have a relatively low practical value for his future career compared with Chinese and English and appeared to possess unclear Japanese self-image in the distant future. Thus, his learning goal related to the JLPT might not be directly connected to his goals for his life in the distant future. In fact, when asked whether they thought they would use Japanese in the future when in high school, six out of twelve learners clearly stated that they did not believe they would use the language, whereas only three participants reported that they did. Pilho's comment below is emblematic of the six who said no:

I: その当時、日本語を将来使うと思っていましたか？
S: いいえ、ぜんぜん。これ（日本語）は趣味としか考えてなかったので。日本語で大学に入学するとも思っていませんでした。

[I: At that time, did you think you would use Japanese in the future?
S: No. Not at all. I thought that Japanese was just a hobby. I did not think that I would major in Japanese.]

Therefore, while in high school, many Korean informants appeared to perceive Japanese language learning as a short-term goal connected primarily, if not only, to their current activities/hobbies.

Hoyle and Sherrill (2006: 1692) suggest that 'possible selves in the near future should be richer in detail but less centred on goals than possible selves in the distant future'. Thus, Anbok's short-term goal, which was connected to his current life activity (study for JLPT), was vivid and thus likely to serve as a powerful motivator for learning Japanese. Although there has been no common definition of *short term* and *long term* in prior research on motivation, the present study defines the short-term future L2 self as one's future self-image within the period of one's current study programme, whereas the long-term future L2 self is taken to be one's future self-image beyond the short-term period. That is to say, if a high school student's future English self-image is connected to a higher grade at school, it can be categorized as a short-term future self-image. If he/she envisages him/herself as majoring in English at university, it can be classified as a long-term future self-image.

Initial motivation to study Japanese at university

All participants decided to continue Japanese language learning at the tertiary level. Table 3.2 shows the reasons they gave for their continued study. First of all, five out of twelve learners regarded their interest in Japanese (pop) culture/language as one of the major reasons for the continuation. For instance, Minseop claimed as follows:

> After the university entrance exam, when we have to decide our university, I was told by my teacher to 'do what you want to do'. I decided to choose Japanese because I liked Japanese culture, *anime* and dramas. I had not thought about studying Japanese at university before the exam.

Table 3.2 The Korean participants' reasons to keep studying Japanese at university

Reasons	Number (n = 12)	%
Interest in (pop) culture	3	25
Interest in language	2	17
Recommendation from others	2	17
Good marks	2	17
Improve language skills	1	8
Like learning	1	8
Academic resources	1	8
Academic credentials	1	8
Total	13	

Contrary to expectations, some of the informants were not able to offer a personal reason why they chose to keep studying Japanese at university. For example, Nampyo reported that he chose to study Japanese by a process of elimination, as he did not have any interest in other areas, stating in the first interview that:

> To be honest, I entered this university without a clear goal. We have to choose our university according to the marks we get in the university entrance exam. I entered this university because I thought language might be more useful than other studies for my future.

Two other participants (Gapsang and Hongdae) similarly claimed that they did not have a personal reason for the decision, stating that they were recommended to do so by other people:

> 私、大学の入学（に必要な）成績がぜんぜんないので、「これ（日本語）でお前は学校に入学ができる」と先生から聞いて、「はい、そうですか」と私（は）日本語を勉強し始めました。
>
> [I did not possess sufficient grades to enter university. So, when a teacher said, 'You can enter university through studying Japanese', I said 'Oh, is that so?', and began to study the language.] (*Gapsang*)
>
> [Actually, I was an expert in *kendo*. So, I wanted to major in a *kendo*-related faculty, but I failed the test. When I was thinking that I might not go to university, a Mayor of A city said to me 'How about going to B University? I will give you a recommendation letter' … Then, I thought that the major which is related to *kendo* might be Japanese. That's all.] (*Hongdae*)

Ultimately, current interests in Japanese (pop) culture/language, recommendations from others and good marks (i.e. successful prior experience with learning Japanese) appear to play important roles in the participants' decisions to keep studying Japanese after transitioning from high school to university.

Extrinsic goals

After entering university, many Korean participants said that they came to have less time to enjoy Japanese pop culture than when they were in high school. Instead, the participants appeared to place greater importance on the goals set out by the university (e.g. graduation requirements and/or getting top marks). The participants can be roughly divided into two groups. The first consists of three participants who, at the outset of university, did not have any clear aim to study Japanese. Rather, they had to take it because they received low marks on the entrance exam, causing them to miss out on their first choice of major. The second group consists of the other nine students, who chose to study Japanese because of a personal interest in the language. The goals expected by the university appear to have had a strong impact on both groups of students. For the former group, attaining a required test score necessary for graduation seemed to be the main goal motivating their Japanese study. Hongdae, for instance, reported as follows:

> I: Do you have motivation now?
> S: Yes, I do.
> I: Why did your motivation increase?
> S: In order to graduate.
> I: How hard do you study Japanese, now?
> S: Three or four hours a day, apart from Japanese class ...
> I: What is your goal for learning Japanese?
> S: To get the JPT marks necessary for graduation.

Since Hongdae's current dream is to establish a company, he seems to concentrate on achieving his short-term goal (i.e. a required JPT score) in order to capitalize on the investment of time and effort so far to help achieve his long-term dream.

As for the latter group, however, in some cases there seems to be a conflict between their personal interests and the external goals imposed by the institute. For example, after entering the university, Cheonga's enthusiasm for learning Japanese derived from her personal interests (e.g. appreciation of TV dramas, *anime* and pop songs) had reduced, partly due to the pressure from the university to increase her JPT score. When asked about her learning experience of Japanese in the university, she explained as follows:

> I am under pressure from professors to increase my JPT score ... My interest in learning Japanese has decreased. In the past I was interested in the language and had a passion to be good at it. But, now, I feel pressured. I often think that I have to increase my [JPT] test score and feel the pressure to take the test. I've begun to feel that I don't want to take the test.

One of the prerequisites for a future L2 self-image to serve as an effective motivator is for the ideal and ought-to selves to complement each other (Dörnyei 2009). However, Cheonga's ideal self-image as a Japanese user does not seem to be in harmony with her *ought-to* self-representation, which is derived from goals imposed by her university. Thus, while an externally imposed goal can sometimes be an effective motivational force, it can negatively influence the maintenance of intrinsic interests and ideal L2 self-images of learners who already have personal interests in the target language/culture.

Attainment of goals

While all the participants were pursuing the external, short-term goals demanded by the university, some participants expressed a lack of long-term goals for learning Japanese. Anbok, for example, had already passed the highest level of the JLPT (N1) in a relatively short period of time when he was a high school student. Since he has already achieved his major goal to study Japanese, his intention to continue studying Japanese appears to have decreased. By the first year of his study, he was looking for an alternative long-term goal as expressed in the following interview extract:

> I: 卒業後、何をしたいですか？
> S: それが一番問題です。先生のみんなから聞かれる質問ですけど「日本語を学んで一体どうやってみたい」と。ぼくはいつも「そう言われても困ります」と（答えます）-。いまゴールがなくて、本当に大変です。誰か僕にゴールをください！いま日本語を学んで、やる気がないというか。

> [I: What do you want to do after you graduate?
> S: This is the biggest issue. The question I am asked by all of my teachers is 'What do you want to do with Japanese?' I always answer like, 'Asking me that doesn't help'. I am in a really tough situation as I don't have any goal. Can somebody please give me a goal! I am not motivated to learn Japanese now.]

Another participant (Pilho) also reported similar experiences of declining motivation after he achieved his desired test scores on the JLPT and JPT. He described his change in learning motivation after obtaining the test score as follows:

> 今は点数もある程度上がったし、Ｎ１もとったし、もう（日本語の勉強を）そんな頑張る必要はないかなと（思います）。... 今、（ゴールが）何かなくなったというか。もとは、JPT900と、N1を取ること（がゴール）でしたけど、今回(それらを)全部取れたので、ゴールはな

くなっています。新しいゴールは見つからず。このまま卒業になるんじゃないかなと思っています。

[Now I think that I don't need to study Japanese hard, as my test marks increased and I took N1 ... I, kind of lost my goals? My previous goals were attaining a mark of 900 on the JPT and passing N1, but I did all of that, so my goals are gone. I can't find any new goals either. I'm thinking I might end up just graduating like this [without Japanese-related goals].]

Although both Anbok and Pilho were advanced learners of Japanese, they did not express a personal goal for learning Japanese after graduation. Thus, some Korean learners may be able to achieve short-term goals for learning Japanese (e.g. test scores) in relatively short periods, which will lead to their motivational enhancement. However, they also tend to struggle to set long-term goals, which contributes to their motivational attrition.

Development of ideal Japanese self

The data also indicates that some Korean informants' future Japanese self-guides have developed since they entered university, especially for the career domain. While there was only one participant (Junha) who imagined himself using Japanese in future employment while still a high school student, in the first interview, eight participants envisioned career-related Japanese selves, though the degree of vividness seems to differ considerably. Additionally, five participants claimed that they could envisage themselves communicating with Japanese friends (interpersonal domain), while eight were able to imagine future self-representations in which they enjoy Japanese media (leisure domain). This evolution of future self-images is probably due to the fact that the participants had a wide range of Japanese-related experiences in and outside of the classroom as they majored in Japanology. This may have helped them develop future self-concepts as Japanese learners/users. Furthermore, their perspectives may have also generally broadened as they grew older.

Strictly speaking, an ideal L2 self may be revised every time it is activated, because possible selves are 'particularly sensitive to those situations that communicate new or inconsistent information about the self' (Markus and Nurius 1986: 956). However, the present study aims to capture relatively broad changes or revisions of one's self-guides. To that end, a perspective of time scale of possible selves (Hoyle and Sherrill 2006) appears to be useful. For instance, when Oyeon was in high school, she studied Japanese hard because of her strong wish to obtain a higher-level certificate of JLPT and seemed to possess a Japanese self-guide in the near future linked to the test (education domain; obtaining academic credentials). However, despite her high level of Japanese proficiency, she reported that she could not imagine herself using Japanese for other domains of her future life. It was only after entering the university that she started to think about her life in the distant future. When asked about her future course, she claimed that she is now able to envision herself using Japanese for her future job (career domain):

> I: 仕事の目標はありますか？
> S: 研究者も好きなんですけど、やっぱり外国の人と話すことが好きなので、貿易と言うか通訳に関する会社とか（を考えています）。
>
> [I: Do you have any career-related goals?
> S: I would like to become a researcher, but I also like to talk with foreigners. So, I'm thinking of things like trading companies or companies related to translating.]

Oyeon's future Japanese self-guide seemed to have expanded from an existing short-term future self-image linked to obtaining a JLPT certificate to a self-image which is connected to the distant future employment, though both L2 selves are not very clear at this point.

However, there are also examples which show that the participants did not expand their existing L2 selves to other domains between high school and university. For instance, since Anbok attained the sufficient JLPT score when he was in high school, he is not required to take the test at his university. By achieving the short-term goal (N1), Anbok's ideal Japanese self, which was linked to the education domain (obtaining academic credentials), was integrated into his current self-concept and thus eliminated from the repertoire of his future self-concepts. After the achievement, his future self-guide did not seem to be revised upwardly. This point will be further discussed later.

I want to study Japanese 'if needed': Intentions to continue studying Japanese

As for the Korean participants' future motivation, my analysis found that their intention to sustain the study of Japanese after graduation was relatively weak, despite that they learned the language as a compulsory part of their university major. When asked about how long they would continue to study Japanese after graduation, five out of twelve participants claimed that they would learn the language if they had a chance to learn or if it was needed for their future job. Cheonga responded as follows:

S: I think I need to study Japanese until graduation.
I: How about after graduation?
S: If there is a chance to use Japanese after graduation, I think I would like to study the language more.

The informants appeared to believe that Japanese would not necessarily be used in their future employment. In addition, two participants (Junha and Minseop) claimed that they might stop learning Japanese but would continue learning English throughout their lives as a career language. Minseop stated, 'I will stop studying Japanese if I quit the IT job. But, I will continue studying English even after I quit the job in order to get another job. There is a huge gap between people who can speak English and people who cannot'. Minseop's comment reflects that the informants might give English a higher priority than Japanese in their future life due to English being viewed as beneficial for a wider range of careers. More detailed analysis on the motivational relationship between Japanese and English will be provided in the following section.

However, four out of twelve informants expressed their desire to continue studying Japanese for a long time, even throughout the rest of their lives. Two participants, Oyeon and Daebeon, stated that they will sustain conscious study of the language, whereas two, Anbok and Bosun, said that they will keep learning/using the language as a 'hobby'. Not all of the four participants had a clear goal for learning Japanese. However, they all did tend to have a great curiosity about the Japanese language. For example, Anbok explained that he will continue with Japanese because he was interested in Japanese classics and *haiku*, which represents his intellectual curiosity. The other informant, Oyeon, claimed that '日本語は死ぬまでやりたいと思って（います）[I would like to study Japanese until die]', which indicates her high levels of passion for learning the language.

Learning experience of English

The Korean participants' English learning experiences are, in general, quite different from their experiences with Japanese. Distinct concepts for Japanese and English seemed to begin as early as high school. For example, one of the most prominent characteristics of the informants' goals for learning English when they were in high school was that the language was linked to their employment in the distant future. However, these future goals often did not subsume visions but related to a general social expectation of a degree of English competence. One of the participants (Nampyo) reported as follows:

I: In high school, did you think that you would use English in the future?
S: Because English is a shared language, I thought that it is always necessary to learn, even if you do not have a clear goal.
I: Did you think you would use English for your career?
S: Yes. At that time, I thought it is necessary for my career. Because, in Korea, English is recognized as a compulsory.

In association with the heavy emphasis on TOEIC in Korean society, there is a widespread belief among young Koreans that English is important for career development (Lyons 2014). Since English is a socially recognized prerequisite for future success, the participants may envisage possible selves who will be using English for their job regardless of their current language competence or their views of their selves as English learners/users. In general, the participants' future goals as English learners connected to the distant future did not seem to involve clear visions and consequently had limited motivational power.

In addition to the long-term future goals, the participants also seemed to possess short-term future goals for English. Since English is one of the subjects required for university entrance examination, they were likely to imagine possible future selves which are related to the upcoming test. The following comment from Pilho confirms that he had a concrete and short-term goal as an English learner, which is connected to the education domain (obtaining academic credentials):

目の前にある大学入学試験のために英語を勉強するのが第一の至急な問題でしたので、それしか考えていませんでした。将来（英語を）使うとはあんまり考えていませんでした。

[Because studying English for the university entrance exam was the most urgent problem, it was all I thought about. I did not really think about using the language in the future.]

Importantly, the construction of the participants' future English goals, which is related to university entrance as well as employment, were, in many cases, influenced by social expectation or beliefs. When asked about the impact of other people on her study of English, Cheonga also replied as follows:

I: Who encouraged you to study English?
S: There are not any particular people who did it, but it was because of the atmosphere ... There was an atmosphere in society that it's just natural to study English. So, I thought I had to.

As the above interview quote indicates, many Korean informants' goals for learning English can be interpreted as *ought-to English selves*.

Despite the fact that only two participants were studying English at the time the interview was conducted, many of them still claimed that they imagine future English selves. After high school, however, the domain of their English self-images had been relatively limited to the career domain. This simplicity and stability of the self-concept is partly because they have had little chance to explore their future English speaking/using selves. Hardly any study has investigated one's self-image in a language that one is currently not learning. However, it would be fair to say that the Korean participants' English self-guides do exist, though they may not be activated frequently.

Relationship between languages: Japanese as a preliminary language to English

Domain of L2 self

One's foreign language self-concept can vary in different learning contexts and is strongly influenced by demographic factors such as gender, race, culture and age (e.g. Mercer 2011; Kormos, Kiddle and Csizér 2011). The present study adapts a concept of *domain of possible selves* (Unemori, Omoregie and Markus 2004) in order to analyze various aspects of the informants' future self-concepts. In my earlier study (Nakamura 2015), which focused on Australian university students' future Japanese self-concept and motivation, participants' L2 self-guides were categorized into one of four domains of future life: *interpersonal*, *education*, *career* and *extracurricular*. Since the focus of the present study is also university Japanese language learners, I decided to utilize this categorization as a starting point for the analysis. However, there were comments which are not able to be classified into any of these domains or subcategories. As a result, the categorization was modified to accommodate these statements. The *extracurricular* domain was renamed as *leisure* domain, and two new subcategories (*obtaining academic credentials* and *access to academic resources*) were added to the education domain. Table 3.3 shows the domains of the Korean participants' projected future L2 use.

Table 3.3 The Korean participants' projected future L2 use

Domains and Subcategories	English	Japanese	Examples
Interpersonal			
Friends	2	5 (1)	I think when I study in Japan, I will have Japanese friends and sometimes call them and stuff. (*Ihyeong*)
Leisure			
Travelling abroad		1	日本くらいはさすがに（家族と）一緒に行きたいと思います。その時でも日本語を使いたい。 [I would like to travel to Japan with my family. I would like to use Japanese when I do.] (*Anbok*)
Enjoying pop culture	3	8	Because I like playing games even now, I may buy a PlayStation and play games in Japanese in the future. (*Ihyeong*)
Career			
Desired Job	7 (1)	8 (1)	I think I will use Japanese for marketing, in order to make good contracts and achieve good results for each company. (*Daebeon*)
Education			
Obtaining academic credentials	(1)	1 (5)	いつかは必ずＪＰＴの990点を取って、「ここまで勉強したよ」って胸を張って言いたいです。 [I would like to obtain a mark of 990 on the JPT and proudly claim 'I studied very well'.] (*Oyeon*)
Study abroad plan		2 (2)	交換留学をしてみて日本での生活をしながら、日本でいろいろな経験をして、…と思っているんですけど、 [As an exchange student, I would like to […] live and have various experiences in Japan.] (*Oyeon*)
Access to academic resources	1	1	Because I wanted to study art, I thought learning many languages would be beneficial for my study of art. (*Cheonga*)
Total	13 (2)	26 (9)	

*The numbers in ( ) represent goals/objects

The number in each subcategory in the table indicates the number of informants who provided the references. It partly reflects their future English and Japanese self-representations that they possessed at the time of the first interview. Many of them seemed to have a variety of future Japanese selves which cover different domains, whereas the domain of their English self-guides was relatively limited to the career domain.

It should be noted that, however, the actual boundary between the domains may be vague. Further, distinct L2 self-images are more likely to overlap or synthesize across boundaries. For instance, a learner's future Japanese self-image of studying at a Japanese university (i.e. *study abroad plan*: education domain) may include a vision in which she/he makes friends with Japanese students (i.e. *friends*: interpersonal domain). Also, learners appear to vary in terms of the complexity of their self-concepts, with some students providing detailed self-descriptions and others being more global in their descriptions. It is possible that some participants may actually have less developed future self-concepts than other individuals in particular domains. Alternatively, individual variation in the depth and complexity of self-descriptions across domains may stem from individuals' differing levels of capacity for depicting themselves in the domains. In any case, the table does not necessarily represent the whole picture of the participants' future English and Japanese self-concepts.

In addition, it was sometimes difficult to clarify the difference between domain-specific goals/objects and the related self-guides. In the data, there is evidence of goals expressed about a specific domain. For example, goals for English in the career domain did not always coincide with expressions of self-representations within the domain. That is, goals may not always entail visions. Although goals and visions are similar in directing toward future states, they are qualitatively different concepts (Dörnyei 2014). Unlike an abstract and cognitive concept of a goal, a vision subsumes both a goal and tangible images related to achieving the goal. In other words, a vision is the goal that 'the learner has made by adding to it the imagined reality of the actual goal experience' (Dörnyei 2014: 12). While recognizing that the participants' learning goals have the potential to become visions, I have tried to classify the participants' statements according to where the learner places the emphasis (i.e. on the cognitive goal or the future self-image) and consulted with peers regarding the classification. Still, there is always some degree of subjectivity when making classifications of this type, and it is possible that another researcher may have classified an instance differently. Table 3.3 should therefore be taken as an illustration to help visualize and compare the participants' goal/L2 self rather than a hard categorization.

A number of studies which investigated learners' motivation across multiple languages (e.g. Dörnyei and Chan 2013; Henry 2011, 2014) have reported a negative motivational impact of L2 English on additional languages in simultaneous learning situations, where learners often come under pressure to allocate time and cognitive resources to two different competing demands. The present study, however, attempts to reveal the motivational relationship between Japanese and English in a context where English is not taught. In this context, it is likely that an individual's future self-guide as an English learner/user may not be activated frequently. As four participants commented, the study of Japanese can have nothing to do with that of English (e.g. Pilho's comment that 'Japanese and English are completely different things'). Many learners appeared to perceive the foreign languages as qualitatively different in terms of the concept of language and their self-view as an L2 learner/user. Nevertheless, some evidence did imply motivational relationships between Japanese and English.

Pressure not to study Japanese but to study English

First of all, for some students there seems to be a negative relationship between the study of Japanese and that of English. Four participants claimed that their study of Japanese has sometimes been weighed against that of English, and they have come under pressure not to study Japanese from others (e.g. parents, teachers and friends). For example, unlike most of the participants, Oyeon was in favour of studying English when she was a high school student. However, she has become more motivated to study Japanese because of her strong interest in the language itself, and her proficiency level of Japanese exceeded that of English. As a result, some people close to her stopped supporting her study of Japanese. She stated as follows:

今は日本語より英語（の能力が）より低いから、風当たりがひどいんです。… 親戚とか家は英語の勉強している人が多くて、「あなたも英語が上手になれば良いのに。成長が止まったよ。日本語ばかり伸びてるじゃない」って（言います）。

[I am being strongly criticized by others because my current proficiency in English is lower than that in Japanese ... There are a lot of people who study English among my relatives and family members, and they say, 'You could be much better at English. Your progress in English has stopped. Only your Japanese is improving'.]

Despite the criticism by parents and relatives who encouraged her to concentrate on developing English proficiency, Oyeon spends more time and effort in studying Japanese. In addition, she is seeking to balance three languages that she is currently learning, as she described the allocation of time as '70 per cent for Japanese, 20 per cent for English and the rest of the time for Mandarin'. Thus, in the Korean context, even though it is not a simultaneous learning context, many Japanese language learners may face a social pressure not to study the language but to study English, forcing them to find a balance between the two.

However, the relationship between Japanese and English is not entirely negative, as there is evidence which demonstrates that some participants conceive of their study of Japanese as useful for their subsequent study of English. That is, not only is Japanese perceived as an easy second language but it can also be a preliminary goal to a more important goal, which is often related to English. For example, Junha considers studying Japanese as a major subject as a step to achieving his primary goal of being a diplomat. He explained his future plan as follows:

I: 卒業後、何をしたいですか？
S: 外交部。国家の外交を担当する機関がありますね。そこに入って外交の仕事をしたいです。…そうするために日本学科に来ました。…私は日本学科の生徒ですけども、あまりにも深く入り込まないで、点数をもらって、日本の方々と会話ができる程度になったらやめて、他の外国語を勉強したいと思います。

[I: What do you want to do after graduation?
S: Ministry of Foreign Affairs. There is a department that takes charge of foreign affairs. I would like to work for it as a diplomat … To do that, I entered the department of Japanology … Although I belong to the department of Japanology, I won't devote myself to it deeply. Rather, after receiving my marks and achieving a level [of Japanese] where I am able to communicate with Japanese people, I want to study other foreign languages.]

In contrast to the study of Japanese, Junha added that he will spend a 'lifetime' on the study of English. Thus, the study of Japanese, in which he will be able to achieve a desired level of proficiency in a relatively short period of time, allows him to spend more time and energy for the study of 'other foreign languages', such as English.

Anbok also considers Japanese as a basis to study English, as it will provide linguistic knowledge and L2 learning experiences. The following quote best describes his choice of foreign languages in the high school and the university:

> 高校の先生が、「英語が難しかったら、ほかの外国語を学んで、その勉強した経験を生かして英語を始めたら-前より易しく進められる」と（言いました）。… 日本語を（専攻）した理由も、語順が同じでわかり易いと聞きましたから。日本語を終わったから、英語をしようと今考えています。

[My high school teacher said, 'If studying English is difficult for you, you can study another language first. Then, you will find it easier to study English because of your previous learning experience with the other language' … The reason why I majored in Japanese is because I heard that the language is easy to learn since it has the same word order as Korean. Because I have finished the study of Japanese, now I am thinking of giving English a try.]

Anbok seemed to perceive gaining a high level of Japanese proficiency as an accessible, short-term future goal which enabled him to prepare to study English.

Ushioda (1998: 83) claimed that language learners in institutional settings generally have multiple goals and that motivation for learning a language is not independent of motivation for other areas of learning. The current study confirms this argument and shows that some participants possess differing goals for Japanese and English with different time scales, allocating their time and effort between these goals. A recent study by Lyons (2014) reported on an English learner in a Korean university who set a series of immediate goals to study English (e.g. getting a high TOEIC score, gaining work experience abroad) in order to realize a more important end goal related to English (being a journalist or a translator). In contrast, some Korean informants of the present study attempted to achieve a short-term goal relating to Japanese while simultaneously pursuing long-term aims related to English. They may see their Japanese goals as a preliminary step, which helps set and realize other (important and long-term) goals. Within an L2 self framework, since Japanese is perceived as an accessible and achievable foreign language, it may be easier for the Korean participants to imagine and realize successful L3 (Japanese) self-images, which allows them to possess distant L2 (English) self-guides beyond the attainment of proximal L3 selves.

Cooperative L2 selves

Although the number was quite limited, there were examples which indicate that different foreign languages are cooperative in the construction of the informants' future self-image. When a learner possesses a clear future vision which requires multiple languages, distinct self-guides for different languages can be synthesized to construct a more elaborated self-image. Interestingly, despite the fact that the participants were specializing in Japanology, two of them (Oyeon and Junha) have a clear future English self-image, which is connected to their Japanese self-guides. For instance, Junha, was studying English in addition to Japanese. He had an ideal future self-image in which he works at the Korean embassy. The following comment implies that he also planned to study other European languages to enhance his career prospects:

> I: 将来の仕事を考えたとき、どんな言葉を使うと思いますか？
> S: ヨーロッパのフランス語とかイギリス英語を使うと思います。フランス語とかドイツ語、スペイン語も勉強したいです。日本語も。
>
> [I: When you think about your future career languages, what languages do you think you might use?
> S: I think I will use European languages, such as French and English. I would like to study French, German and Spanish. Japanese, too.]

Junha seemed to believe that all the languages he has learnt and will learn are positively linked to his future career. These language selves may complement each other to construct a future image of a self who can speak a number of languages interchangeably. Also, having an established self-image as a successful L2 user may help him to imagine this extended to other languages in future. Thus, when different ideal L2/L3/L4 selves share a common domain of one's future life, these self-concepts may be synthesized to construct a multilingual vision within the domain.

Chapter summary

Many Korean informants' initial driving force in Japanese language learning was their interest in the language/culture (e.g. pop culture), which also became a chief reason for their interest in learning the language at their university. Their future self-images as Japanese users, however, did not always have a motivational power. When in high school, many of them might possess personal and short-term future self-images as Japanese users/learners which were connected to their everyday life, such as appreciation of Japanese pop culture (leisure domain) and academic credentials (education domain). At their university, however, they are instructed to focus on extrinsic goals. While there are plenty of opportunities to learn the language at the university, many informants have few chances to communicate with people in Japanese outside of the classroom. Further, some of them expressed that English plays a more important role than Japanese in their future employment. This means that they envisioned ought-to English selves which are linked to the career domain. These factors might all have a negative impact on constructing the Korean informants' long-term learning goals or ideal Japanese self-representations in the distant future, which is reflected in their weak intentions to continue studying Japanese after graduation. These findings from the Korean first round interview will be re-examined through comparing them with those from the Australian interview in the following chapter.

4

'Japanese is difficult, but I don't want to stop.' Motivation and future self-images of Australian learners

This chapter investigates the Australian Japanese language learners' motivational development during the period from the commencement of their Japanese study to the time of the first interview. Similar to the previous chapter, I first describe the informants' L2 learning experiences when in high school and university. After that, the complex relationship between their motivation for learning Japanese and for other languages will be analyzed. Since the Australian learners may have quite different learning experiences than their Korean counterparts, a comparison between these two groups of learners will constructively shed light on how different social contexts affect and shape motivation.

Background of the Australian participants

Nine female and five male students agreed to participate in the present study. The first interview was conducted at an Australian university in March 2015. Most (10/14) of the interviews were carried out in English, but four students preferred to have the interview conducted in Japanese. Table 4.1 illustrates the background of the participants. The participants were categorized into one of three groups according to their linguistic/cultural background: 1) *Monolingual*, 2) *Bilingual (East-Asian-background)* and 3) *Bilingual (Non-East-Asian-background)*. The first group comprises six native English speakers born and brought up in monolingual families in Australia. The second group comprises eight participants who grew up in East-Asian background families, all of whom possess their own heritage languages (Mandarin, Cantonese, Teochew and Korean). Xin is an international student from Malaysia, who arrived in

Table 4.1 Background of Australian participants

Name (pseudonym)	Age	Major at University/ Year Level	L1	L2/Formal Study	L3/Formal Study	L4/Formal Study	L5/Formal Study
1) Monolingual							
1 Laura	20	Arts/2	English	Japanese 5 years (S) 1 year (A) 1 year (U)	Korean 1 year (U)	Mandarin 1 month (U)	
2 Diane	20	Arts/2	English	French 2 years (S)	Japanese 2 years (S) 1 year (A) 1 year (U)		
3 Scott	20	Arts/3	English	Japanese 6 years (S) 1 year (U)	Indonesian 1 month (U)		
4 George	21	Arts/2	English	Japanese 3 years (S) 4 years (U)			
5 Debra	20	Arts/2	English	Japanese 6 years (S) 1 year (U)			
6 Emma	23	Arts/4	English	French 3 years (U)	German 3 years (S)	Japanese 2 years (U)	

2) Bilingual (East-Asian background)

#	Name	Age	Degree/Year	L1	L2	L3	L4	L5
7	Luyue	20	Arts, Science/3	English	Cantonese	Japanese 6 years (S) 3 years (U)	Mandarin- 4 years (S) 1 year (U)	Korean 1 month (U)
8	Shiyi	18	Arts, Law/1	English	Mandarin 3 years (L)	French 6 years (S)	Indonesian 5 years (S)	Japanese 4 years (L) 1 year (U)
9	Jiajie	18	Arts, Engineering/2	English	Teochew	Japanese 13 years (S) 1 year (U)		
10	Yian	19	Arts, Business and Economics/2	English	Mandarin 8 years (S)	Japanese 4 years (S) 2 years (U)	Korean 1 year (U)	
11	Xin	20	Business and Economics/3	English	Mandarin	Malay 12 years (S)	Japanese 2 years (U)	
12	Iseok	23	Arts, Law/3	Korean	English 10 years (S)	Japanese 1 years (S) 2 years (U)	Mandarin 1 year (U)	

3) Bilingual (Non-East-Asian background)

#	Name	Age	Degree/Year	L1	L2	L3	L4
13	Kris	23	Arts/2	English	Greek 10 years (S)	Japanese 2 years (U)	German 6 months (U)
14	Dung	19	Arts/2	Vietnamese	English 13 years (S)	Japanese 6 years (S) 3 years (U)	

*S: primary-high school/ U: university/ A: study abroad / L: government-owned language school

Australia in 2012. Iseok immigrated to Australia when in secondary school. Although these participants were not raised in Australia from birth, they are classified into the second group due to their East-Asian background. The third group is composed of two learners who grew up in families with a linguistic/cultural background other than Australia and East-Asia. Although one of these participants (Dung) classified English as her second language, she claims that she speaks both Vietnamese and English at a native level.

In the table, **bold** type indicates native languages that are spoken at home. Some native languages were acquired exclusively at home, while the others were learnt both at home and school. Although the current study classifies L1, L2, L3 in the order in which the informants learned, for some informants who possess two native languages, it may be difficult to clarify their L1 and L2. In these cases, the language which the informant perceives higher competence is classified as her/his L1, and the other language is categorized as her/his L2 for convenience of explanation. Therefore, it is worth noting that the term 'L2' in the table involves two different meanings. For the informants in Group 1, 'L2' means the first foreign language they studied at school, whereas for most informants in Group 2 and 3, 'L2' represents their heritage language.

All students except one (Emma) studied Japanese at high school or at a private institute before entering university, with the amount of study ranging from a few months to thirteen years. Importantly, eleven out of fourteen students have visited Japan, and six of them have studied in Japanese high schools or university. This is in stark contrast to the Korean context, where only one informant had experienced study in Japan (Chapter 3). The motivational impact of the Australian students' study abroad experiences will be discussed later. At the time of the current study, the Australian informants were all enrolled in the proficient or advanced levels of Japanese. In more specific terms, learners who enrol in the proficient level are expected to have Japanese language ability equal to N4 of JLPT, which ranges from the highest N1 to the lowest N5, and learners who enrol in the advanced level are expected to have Japanese language ability equal to N3 of JLPT.

Learning experience of Japanese

In contrast to their Korean counterparts, the Australian learners had a wider variety of cultural backgrounds and language learning experiences. While the Korean study primarily focused on the participants' *learning* experiences with Japanese and English, the diverse nature of the Australian participants necessitates that characteristics of both the Australian informants' experiences of *learning* and *using* Japanese are investigated.

Interest in Japanese pop culture and language

Most prominently, seven of the participants reported that they enjoyed Japanese pop-culture such as music and *anime*, which is correspondent to the result from the Korean study. For these students, this interest seemed to be the initial force that drove them to study Japanese when in high school. Three of the seven explicitly stated that their interest in pop culture stimulated their interest in the Japanese language, as well as Japanese culture as a whole. For instance, when in high school Jiajie (L1: English, L2: Teochew, L3: Japanese) enjoyed reading Japanese pop idols' blogs, doing so almost every day. In order to understand the contents, he used a computer program, which reads the *kanji* (Chinese characters) and shows the meanings, and developed language skills through this process. Indeed, Jiajie described, 'I started with music, and from the music, I branched out into everything else. So, I think the music just kept me going'. Yian (L1: English, L2: Mandarin, L3: Japanese, L4: Korean) similarly commented, 'Actually at the beginning I was interested in *anime*. But, as I grew up, I really liked Japanese culture. More of the Japanese culture than *anime* itself. So, I am also very interested in the language'.

Although there is a wide diversity in the languages that the Australian participants possess (see Table 4.1), many of them were interested in Japanese language itself. The learners in Group 2, whose heritage languages have more linguistic elements in common with Japanese (e.g. *kanji*) and whose societies share longer histories and cultural philosophical principles like Confucianism and Buddhism, may perceive a smaller linguistic/cultural distance from Japanese than the learners in Group 1 (cf. Matsumoto 2009). For instance, Luyue (L1: English, L2: Cantonese, L3: Japanese, L4: Mandarin, L5: Korean), who speaks Cantonese as a family language, claimed that she became interested in Japanese in primary school 'because it is close to Cantonese' and began to study the language after entering a secondary school which offered Japanese. That is, a perceived linguistic/cultural closeness between her first/heritage language and Japanese seemed to positively influence her decision to commence Japanese study.

Interestingly, however, greater linguistic/cultural distance also showed the potential to contribute to the attractiveness of Japanese. This phenomenon was particularly noted in the statements from the learners from Group 1. For example, Emma (L1: English, L2: French, L3: German, L4: Japanese) learned French when in high school but decided to take an additional second language at university. She provided her reason for choosing Japanese over other options as follows:

> Well, I needed something that was very different from French, because I didn't want to study French and Italian, or French and Spanish, and I have two languages that are very similar ... Japanese was something I was interested in, so.

The quote above shows Emma's decision to choose Japanese as a fourth language was caused by her greater curiosity towards a language which is linguistically distant from her L1/L2.

Inspiring teachers

Another prominent trend is that the participants generally enjoyed their study of Japanese in high school, with these experiences influencing their decisions to pursue further study of Japanese. Positive experiences with high school teachers appeared to have an especially positive impacts, as four of the participants regarded their teachers as the most significant person in their learning history of Japanese. For example, when asked about his Japanese learning experiences at high school, Scott (L1: English, L2: Japanese, L3: Indonesian) stated that:

> And the Japanese teachers were my favourite teachers. They were so nice to us, so, like gave more motivation to study. They were really nice. They were, like, they were kind of like mothers ... They were really good friends, they always bring birthday cakes on the birthdays.

As his phrase 'like mothers' shows, for Scott, the teachers were perceived more like family members or friends than just language teachers, providing support and influence that continued outside the classroom. Similarly, Yian said that she studied Japanese hard because of a high school teacher who devoted his time and energies to providing her with various learning opportunities apart from the normal class, and Laura (L1: English, L2: Japanese, L3: Korean, L4: Mandarin) also reported that her high school teacher had a significant impact on her study of Japanese:

> I: その当時、日本語を将来使うと思っていましたか？
> S: Brown 先生の話を聞く前は、やはり思わなかったんです。この社会には、大学に行くのは、なんか、医者になりたいと、Go

to university, study Medicine. 大学に行って、Study Engineering, become an engineer. だけど、大学に行って（第二）言語を勉強すると何になる？という話だったんですけど、Brown先生が言語を話せると仕事が実はいっぱいありますということを、よく彼女は自分の生徒だけじゃなくて、その高校全体に...教えてくれました。

[I: At that time, did you think you might use Japanese in the future?
S: I didn't think so before listening to Ms Brown's talk. In this society, if one wants to be a doctor, people think 'Go to university, study medicine', or 'Go to university and study engineering, become an engineer'. But, if one studies a [second] language, what can she/he become? Ms Brown often explained ... not only to his own students but also to a whole school that if one can speak a second language, then one can have a variety of jobs.]

The extract presented above indicates that the teacher helped her students envision their future life with foreign languages. Indeed, Laura commented that 'I used to think that I want to become like the teacher (Ms Brown)'. Therefore, for some participants, the high school teachers might be like parents who encourage their study of Japanese, and for the others, they might be regarded as role models of their ideal self. This is in marked contrast to the Korean context, where none of the students explicitly expressed the importance of their high school teachers. This is not to say that all Australian students viewed their teachers positively. Luyue, for instance, said that her high school teacher was 'very strict'. However, she also recognized the significance of the teacher in her learning history of Japanese and stated that her current language proficiency level is largely due to the teacher.

Sojourn experience in Japan

Among the thirteen learners who have visited Japan, five had study abroad experiences ranging from three months to one year. Four of these five (Laura, Debra, Diane and Shiyi) studied in Japan when in high school, and one (Yian) did so after entering the university. In contrast, although eight out of the twelve Korean learners had visited Japan, only one of them studied in Japan as an exchange student when he was in university. Most of the five Australian informants reported changes in their attitudes towards Japanese culture and language during and after their period of study abroad. For instance, Shiyi

(L1: English, L2: Mandarin, L3: French, L4: Indonesian, L5: Japanese) realized that her proficiency in Japanese improved after a three-month stay in Osaka when in high school, she described in the following extract:

> But after [the study abroad], I, kind of, started thinking more in Japanese, thinking not to translate, but speak only in Japanese. Yeah, so there was something change, I think. Because friends around me were speaking Japanese. So, I processed in Japanese rather than translating from English to Japanese as much as I could.

In addition to changes in language proficiency, three of the participants also reflected that their stay in Japan broadened their horizons and provided them with a better understanding of Japanese people/culture. Diane (L1: English, L2: French, L3: Japanese), for instance, studied at a high school in Mie Prefecture for one year. She looked back on her experience in Japan as follows:

> Before I went to exchange, I thought Japanese are very, very polite, quite reserved, in their personalities. And then, I went to school, and the girls at the school were just crazy. I completely changed my view. Also, I was there during the big earthquake, tsunami. And, yeah, and I was just amazed how much the Japanese people value community, and they just kind of go together, as a country. Cause I was seeing quite individualistic and very focused on business. But then, when disaster hits, they all pull together and everyone helped each other.

Diane reported that in addition to her experiences at the high school and during the natural disaster, her life experiences with two host families were also significant events in her learning history of Japanese. The words in the above quote such as 'changed' and 'amazed' show the importance of her various first-hand experiences in Japan in expanding her horizons. That is, she gained significantly more awareness of, and empathy for, Japanese culture/people. Interestingly, while similar stories of personal growth were also provided by two other Australian informants (Scott and Emma) who had just travelled in Japan, none of the Korean counterparts who had visited Japan made similar comments.

Japanese as a long-term goal

With respect to the participants' future L2 self-guides, a number of the participants' statements indicated that when in high school they possessed ideal Japanese selves linked to a variety of domains of life in the distant future, though the degree of vividness seems to vary markedly. The following quote describes that Jiajie (L1: English, L2: Teochew, L3: Japanese) envisioned a job-related future self-image in which he uses Japanese as an engineer:

> When I was at high school, I was thinking about doing engineering in the future. So, I think engineering jobs are hard to find here, but it might be a bit easier in Japan. So, maybe I could get a job in Japan.

Although Jiajie's ideal self-image as a Japanese user did not seem to be very clear, he at least had a long-term goal for learning the language, which can strongly motivate his learning.

Initial motivations to study Japanese at university

Australian participants' reasons for continuing with Japanese at the university were considerably different from those of the Korean informants. As shown in Table 4.2, while four Korean learners were not able to provide positive reasons to keep studying Japanese at university (see Chapter 3), all the Australian participants had at least one personal reason and generally reported more positive and intrinsic motives to continue with Japanese at university. It should be noted that there is no clear-cut boundary between the categories in Table 4.2. Further, given reasons overlapped in many cases, which confirms

Table 4.2 The Australian participants' reasons to keep studying Japanese at university

Reasons	Australia (N=14)		Korea (N=12)	
	Number	%	Number	%
Improve language skills	5	36	1	8
Don't want to waste	5	36	–	–
Interest in language	4	29	2	17
Future career	3	21	–	–
Like learning	3	21	1	8
Study in Japan	1	7	–	–
Interest in (pop) culture	1	7	3	25
Good marks	1	7	2	17
Recommendation from others	–	–	2	17
Academic resources	–	–	1	8
Academic credentials	–	–	1	8
Total	23		13	

Ushioda's (1998) argument that L2 learners have multiple and complex motives for studying a language. Nonetheless, I believe that the table helps clarify and compare the participants' decision to study Japanese at the university in these contexts.

First of all, the Australian participants' interests in Japanese language and culture have been shown to play an important role in their decision to keep learning Japanese at the university, which is congruent with the Korean data (see Chapter 3). As has been shown in Table 4.2, five participants chose to study Japanese because of their interest in the language itself, and one (Iseok) claimed that it was due to his interest in the pop culture. Iseok (L1: Korean, L2: English, L3: Japanese, L4: Mandarin), who speaks Korean as a family language, was interested in Japanese language and pop culture when in high school. Similar to some Korean informants, he taught himself the language and perceived it as an easy language. He reported that at that time Japanese was perceived as a 'hobby' as he became familiar with the language through pop culture (e.g. *manga*, pop songs). He explained why he changed his second major from science to Japanese as follows:

私がはじめて大学に入るときは、サイエンスと法律を（専攻として）やっていました。でも、その時サイエンスがとっても適性に合わなくて、変わりましたよ。…ちょっとサイエンスであんまりcreditをもらえませんでしたので心配でした。で、一番自分にやさしい科目をやろうかと思って、日本語を選びました。「自分、できるから。」って感じで。

[When I entered university, I was majoring in science and law. But, I found that I didn't have an aptitude for science, so I changed my major … I worried about my major because I was not successful in earning credits in science. So, I decided to learn the easiest subject for me, and chose Japanese. I thought like, 'I can do it'.]

As words such as 'easiest subject' tell us, Iseok's perceived self-confidence in learning Japanese contributed to the decision to study the language at the university. Debra (L1: English, L2: Japanese) also provided a similar statement. She had a positive learning experience in Japan when in high school, and the experience stimulated her deep interest in Japanese. When asked about her reasons for continuing with Japanese at the university, she stated that:

ほかの人と日本語で話すことが楽しいし、毎週チャレンジ（して）、もっと難しいことを勉強するのはいい経験だと思いましたし。あのまあ、ちょっと説明しにくいけど、とにかくすごく大好きだから。

[Because I thought talking with other people in Japanese was fun and that studying more difficult and challenging things every week was a good experience for me. Well, it's a little bit difficult to explain, but, it is because I just like the language very much.]

While Debra does perceive learning Japanese as a 'challenge', she enjoys the challenging aspects of the learning, which in turn, influenced her decision to continue with the language at the tertiary level. The above examples indicate that linguistic/cultural distance between their first/heritage languages and Japanese influenced the informants' study of the language in different ways. That is, when the distance is relatively small, learning Japanese may be conceived as relatively easy work, which positively influences their choice of the language at the university. This trend was also observed in the Korean data. However, when the language distance is larger, it may sometimes cause motivational attrition due to the perceived difficulties in the L2 learning. However, the large distance caused some informants to have a deeper curiosity about the language, which supported their decision to learn the L2 despite its perceived difficulty.

Additionally, the overall tone of the fourteen interviews reflects that the participants' initial interest in Japanese language/culture was triggered by immediate experiences, such as consumption of Japanese pop culture and classroom study and then shifted to more individual curiosity about the language. For instance, Kris (L1: English, L2: Greek, L3: Japanese, L4: German) taught himself Japanese when in high school and started to learn the language officially at a university. He described the shift in his motives to learn the language as follows:

And there are many reasons ... once I study Japanese. Of course, from being very young, I [watched] *anime* and *manga*, and TV, of course ... And so, yeah, my interest began ... But, as I grew up, my reason for wanting to learn Japanese matured a little bit. And I came to love the way Japanese is written, and I specially love the way Japanese sounds. So, I love listening to Japanese. I found [it] very melodic. I think it's a beautiful language.

What we can see from his statement is that Kris has a great curiosity about Japanese language in terms of the way it is 'written' and 'sounds'. This area of interest was not detected in the Korean data. Further, as his learning experience and knowledge about the language has broadened, Kris's curiosity about the language has gradually developed, and this seems to have become a strong driving force in his learning. Thus, it is possible that the Australian learners' interest in Japanese language/culture evolves over time and that this evolution positively influences the commencement of their learning and helps to sustain their engagement.

One of the most significant characteristics in the Australian informants' reasons to study Japanese at the university is their desire to increase their language proficiency, which often reflects their ideal Japanese self-images. As Table 4.2 showed, five of the participants claimed that they decided to keep studying Japanese at the university in order to improve their language skills. Only one Korean informant explicitly offered the same reason. Two participants explained their main reasons for the continuation as follows:

> I wanted to continue from high school. And also I wanted to have more opportunities to improve my writing skills ... I can usually recognize [*kanji*], but it's hard to write sometimes. So, yeah, I thought that it would be good to improve writing and reading. (*Shiyi*)
>
> And I wanted to learn more, I wanted to get better than I was, and I wanted to keep going. (*George*)

The Australian informants, in general, consistently have had the desire to become more fluent in Japanese over time. Scott (L1: English, L2: Japanese, L3: Indonesian) states his ambition as '*perapera ni naritai* (I want to speak fluently)', and George (L1: English, L2: Japanese) comments, 'I want to be fluent 100 percent'. From an L2 self perspective, it would be fair to say that these informants perceive a clear gap between their actual and ideal self-representations as Japanese speaker/user and are motivated to reduce the discrepancy between them.

Desire not to 'waste' previous study

Another prominent reason for the Australian informants to choose to study Japanese at the university is because they did not want to waste the time and effort they had spent learning the language (see Table 4.2). Five of them provided this reason, and again, similar comment was not observed in the Korean data. For instance, Yian claimed, 'Since I had been studying Japanese for so long in the high school, I thought it would be a waste if I suddenly stopped. So, I chose to do Japanese'. These five participants with this view had studied Japanese as an elective subject at their secondary school for a total of three to six years. Furthermore, two of them had studied Japanese as a compulsory subject before they chose it as an elective. Therefore, one can claim that the participants did not want to waste time and energies they had spent in the study of Japanese as an elective subject. However, this claim cannot be fully supported because none of the Korean participants explicitly stated the same reason despite the fact that eight of them had chosen to study Japanese at their high school or taught themselves, ranging from one to eight years.

One possible explanation is that this difference is derived from the degree of difficulty for learning Japanese. For instance, Iseok, the Australian participant who speaks Korean as his mother tongue, decided to choose Japanese as his major subject at the university due to the ease with which he learns the language, and similar statements are extracted from the Korean data (see Chapter 3). Korean native speakers who learn Japanese may be able to compare the learning process of English and that of Japanese because they have learnt English during their school period. This comparison may raise their awareness that the study of Japanese is easier than that of English and thus lead them to believe that losing Japanese proficiency is not a great loss. however, monolingual speakers of English generally need to invest a considerable amount of time and effort in learning Japanese due to the large linguistic/cultural distance, which might result in their comments that they do not want to waste the language. In fact, four out of the five learners who provided statements to that effect belong to Group 1 (the monolingual English background group).

Moreover, all the informants who learnt Japanese in high school took a certificate called the VCE (Victoria Certificate of Education), which is considered to be a pathway to further study at university. As can be imagined, considerable effort is required to obtain the certificate. Therefore, because of the enormous investment in learning Japanese and attaining their high school qualification, they may feel more strongly about the value of their Japanese proficiency and the need to maintain it. In other words, stopping the study and losing Japanese proficiency may be more keenly felt to be a waste of time and effort which hopefully should be avoided. The following interview extract from Scott expresses this view:

> I did not want to, also didn't want to give up what I've spent so much time on ... I guess, the first ... 7, 8, 9, 10, you don't learn very much, you just study pretty much hiragana, katakana. But then, Year 11 and 12, you start learning a lot, and lots of grammar and hand writing essays, and everything. So, I didn't want to just waste of lots of time I spent ... So, I wanted to keep going.

What we can also see here is that these comments imply a fear of losing Japanese. In other words, the reason to continue with Japanese (i.e. because they do not want to waste the language) mirrors their concern about the potential consequence of losing the L2 unless they make conscious efforts to maintain it.

One of the informants, Debra, expressed her fear of losing Japanese language as follows:

（勉強を）やめるのが、ちょっと。絶対にやめたくない。もし忘れて、ちょっと怖いと思います。

[To stop learning the language, it's a bit … I absolutely never want to stop. If I forget it … I think that would be a bit scary.]

One's ideal L2 self is most effective when it is offset by one's feared self in the same domain, because 'future self-guides are most potent if they utilize the cumulative impact of both approach and avoid tendencies' (Dörnyei 2009: 37). Thus, it is possible that some of the Australian informants may have both ideal and feared self-images in a future state, meaning that they are in possession of a great energizing potential.

In a previous study which investigated Australian university students' persistence in studying Japanese, Matsumoto (2009) claimed that Western-background learners of Japanese develop stronger cultural interests than East-Asian background students. This encourages them to further their *investment* in acquiring knowledge about Japan and the Japanese language. In other words, a larger distance between Japanese and their mother tongue/culture (here, English and Australia) may need a larger investment in learning the language. However, because of the increased investment, once a student has achieved a particular level of proficiency in Japanese, they might acquire stronger interests in the language/culture than someone from a more similar linguistic/cultural background. As a result, they are more likely to maintain their study of Japanese (Matsumoto 2009). The current research further argues that one's L2 self-image as a Japanese user/learner is also one of the major driving forces in sustaining one's engagement with learning. As the learners' investment in Japanese increases, they may start to envision not only new ideal Japanese self-representations but also new feared self-images relating to losing their language proficiency, and both of these images can contribute to maintain/further motivation.

Challenging but rewarding

The Australian informants generally reported that the study of Japanese at university was challenging. In the first interview, seven emphasized the differences between their study of Japanese at high school and that at university. For instance, Dung (L1: English, L2: Vietnamese, L3: Japanese) described her learning experience of Japanese at her university as follows:

S: Very difficult. It's very different from [the study of Japanese for] VCE. And it has a lot of content ... So, sometimes I found it's a little bit hard, difficult.
I: Which is more difficult part?
S: *Keigo* (Japanese honorifics) and *kanji*, perhaps.

Despite their perceived difficulties, the seven participants commented that they enjoyed the study of Japanese. For example, Emma (L1: English, L2: French, L3: German, L4: Japanese) explained that she came to enjoy the study of Japanese due to her positive travel experiences in Japan:

But, then I went to Japan at the end of the year, and I loved it. So, that motivated me to go back and study it more. Yeah, and then, ... I got a whole group of friends [in classroom] ... so that's massive motivation to keep going it ... But, since then, I find it much easier.

I: Now do you feel it [Japanese study] is easy?
S: No. By no means. But, I enjoy it. So, it makes it much easier to sit there and study. You know, when I started, I didn't really know anything at all about the Japanese culture. But ... it (Japanese program), a sort of, introduced me all of it and now I love watching Japanese movies and Japanese TV shows. I love them. So, all of that made it easier to get into it.

The above extract indicates that Emma's positive experiences in Japan, relationship with classmates and increasing interest in Japanese pop culture all help increase her enjoyment of Japanese study, which compensates for the difficulty. In addition, compared with their Korean counterparts, none of the Australian informants reported that they had pressure to achieve extrinsic goals (e.g. JLPT), which also seemed to contribute to sustaining their enjoyment in the study of Japanese.

Relationship with Japanese friends/host families

One of the most significant aspects of the Australian informants' usage of Japanese outside of the classroom is the multitude of opportunities they have for communicating with their friends in Japanese. Eight of them said they enjoy consuming Japanese pop culture, such as *anime* and TV shows, which is correspondent with the statements of many Korean participants. However, it is remarkable that eight out of fourteen participants also reported that they currently have at least one Japanese friend to communicate with on a regular basis, as this was true of only three Korean counterparts. Five of the Australian participants made friends with Japanese students who came to Australia for various personal (e.g. homestay or travel) and university-related (e.g. university exchange) experiences. The following interview extracts typify the participants' comments regarding how they make and maintain contact/friendship with native Japanese speakers:

> ええ、ときどきフェイスブックで日本の友達と家族と連絡します。その時は日本語だけ使います。
>
> [Yes, I sometimes communicate with my friends and host family in Japan through Facebook. Then I use only Japanese.] (*Debra*)

> I: Do you have any chance to use Japanese outside of the classroom now?
> S: Yeah, because I'm vice-president of the Japanese club. So, then … I met [Japanese university students from] Tōhoku, Ocha-no-mizu, Ōsaka, Nagoya, Kyūshū. I met all of those students. And I can make friends with them. I've been using it like every day. (*Jiajie*)

Importantly, the participants' various L2 learning and use experiences have a considerable impact on the construction of their ideal L2 selves. For instance, Kris (L1: English, L2: Greek, L3: Japanese, L4: German) claimed that he is able to imagine himself using Japanese not only with his Japanese friends but also with his Australian friends in the future:

> Also, with a large portion of my friends, I envision myself using Japanese, because my many friends I made are in A University and B University. Some friends went to live in Japan, study in Japan.

As his study of Japanese progressed, Kris seemed to start to envisage an ideal self-image in which he communicates with his friends (both Japanese and non-Japanese) in Japanese.

Also, among the four participants who have experience studying in a Japanese high school, three of them have kept in constant touch with their friends or host family. This contact also appears to be an important resource which helps them imagine ideal self-representations as Japanese users. For example, Laura had a one-year study abroad experience in Fukui when in high school. The following interview extract describes how this experience motivates her desire to revisit Japan:

> ああ、また行きたいんです、はい。福井県に留学しましたので、（そこに）戻りたいという、何か帰りたいという（気持ちがあります）。景色を見たくて。人と会いたくて。…何か日本人が道で歩いていると、日本人が近くにいると、シャンプーの匂いがすごくなんか「懐かしい！」という感じかな。誰かがあんぱん買うと、「懐かしい！あんぱん」とか、そういう小さいこと。懐かしいと思って帰りたい。

[Yes, I want to visit Japan again. Since I studied in Fukui, I have a wish to return, and go back there. I want to see the sights and meet people there … When I walk on the street and come across a Japanese person, I can smell the scent of Japanese shampoo, and it just takes me back. When somebody buys an *anpan* [bean-jam bun], I think 'Ohh, yeah, *anpan*!', and little things like that make me remember Japan and want to go back.]

The quote above shows that Laura's long-term exposure to Japan caused not only her feeling of nostalgia, but also a sense of belonging, which is evident from the repetition of the phrase '帰りたい (want to go back)'. Furthermore, her various experiences in Japan enable her to feel, look and even smell Japanese people/society, even when she is living in Australia. Debra, who has studied in Japan for six months, reported a similar desire to live in Japan:

I: 日本語の勉強をこの先どのくらい続けると思いますか？
S: ずっと。年寄りになるまで。そして日本人のように、なんだろう。ライスフィールドで（米を）作りたいです。ずっと田舎で。いまでもやりたい。

[I: How long do you think you will continue to study Japanese?
S: Until I become an old woman. And, just like a Japanese person I want to, what's it called, make a rice field [sic]. In the country, always. I want to do it even now.]

The participants' long-standing relationships with their Japanese friends/families might give them a sense of belonging and strong desire to revisit/live in Japan, which helps them envisage vivid future self-images as Japanese users.

Development of ideal Japanese self

In the interview, all but one of the Australian participants claimed that they would use Japanese for their future career. The following interview extracts from two informants exemplify this trend:

I: What are your goals of studying Japanese?
S: I would really want to work in Japan, or work for trading company in Australia as a translator, or someone that goes between Australia and Japan ... That is kind of one of the things that I would like to do, either for people when they come to Japan, or when Japanese come to Australia. *(Diane)*

I: When you think of your future career, what languages do you think you might use?
S: Just English or Japanese ...
I: I see. In what situations?
S: Talking with co-workers. Like reading instructions for what I am doing. Like making instructions ... *(Jiajie)*

As the above quotes show, the Australian informants tended to express more vivid ideal Japanese selves which are connected to the career domain compared with their Korean counterparts.

I want to study Japanese 'forever': Intentions to continue studying Japanese

As we have already seen, the Australian learners' interests in Japanese language/culture, as well as ideal and feared Japanese self-images derived from their investment in the language, may have been important factors behind their commencement of Japanese at the university. It appears that these elements also result in their strong intention to continue the study for a prolonged period of time. When asked about how long they will study Japanese after the graduation, eight of the informants clearly stated that they want to continue with Japanese for 'a lifetime' or 'forever'. Six of them belong to Group 1 and 3, meaning that they have a non-East-Asian background, whereas the other two participants are from Group 2. Examples of this trend include:

> Forever ... I enjoy reading, and like I enjoy speaking in Japanese, I like the sound, how it sounds. *(Jiajie)*

> Forever. I think so ... I think I'll constantly have to be revising. Cause the culture is always changing, and language is always changing. So, I always have to, feel like, I need to keep up with it. *(Diane)*

> I suppose I don't really have any plan to stop learning Japanese. If I plan on using Japanese in the future as a career, then I would forever be continuing to learn Japanese. *(Kris)*

Five of the eight participants claimed that the main reason they wanted to study Japanese for life is because of an interest in Japanese language/culture as shown in the first quote from Jiajie. However, Jiajie also reported that he can envisage a future Japanese self-image as an engineer (career domain). In the second extract, we can see that Diane's reason to keep studying Japanese is derived from her sense of obligation or feared self-image in which she will lose proficiency in Japanese, as is represented by her use of terms like 'have to' and 'need to'. However, it might be the reflection of her ideal Japanese self-image which is linked to the career (translator), interpersonal (friends) and leisure (playing *koto*) domains of her future life. In the third statement, Kris indicates that his positive future self-image as a Japanese user, which is linked to the career domain, brings about his strong intention, but he also has an intrinsic interest in the language.

Therefore, it seems that various factors are interrelated and contribute to the Australian informants' intention to study Japanese 'forever'. Matsumoto (2009) argued that Australian L2 learners tend to have a larger investment in the learning and develop more interests in the target language/culture due to their larger cultural/linguistic distance from Japan, which helps them continue their study. The current research result supports this assertion. However, the present study further emphasizes the importance of an L2 self-guide in one's persistence in the learning. As far as the Australian participants are concerned, their interests in Japanese language/culture, as well as ideal and feared self-images as Japanese language learners/users, appear to be significant factors in their intention to learn the language 'forever'.

Learning experience of other languages

Six Australian participants studied languages other than English (Mandarin, French, Indonesian, German and Malay) at high school in addition to Japanese. It seems that Australia's multilingual and multicultural environment helps facilitate their study of languages. Yian (L1: English, L2: Mandarin, L3: Japanese, L4: Korean) reported her experience when in high school as follows:

> I have a Korean friend, and every now and then, he talks to me in Korean. But, because I watch Korean dramas, I understand what he says, but I cannot reply. So, it's a kind of one-way. And I reply in English, but he understands. But, anyway, I found that was a kind of inconvenient that he speaks to me [while

I reply back] in another [language]. So, in my free time ... on the internet, I kind of did the internet lessons of Korean.

Although their motives and learning experiences are quite diverse, the Australian participants often stated that they envision these L2s as related to future employment. For instance, consider Emma's (L1: English, L2: French, L3: German, L4: Japanese) reply to the question of if she will use French in the future:

> Yeah, I thought if I became proficient enough ... I might be able to go over there and teach or something.

Among those seven participants who have heritage languages (Cantonese, Mandarin, Teochew, Vietnamese and Greek), three of them studied these languages at school, while the others have learnt them mainly at home. Some reported that they had acquired these languages relatively naturally, while the others said that they had to make a conscious effort to learn them. They provided a number of examples which reflect that these languages are connected to their family members and/or future employment. Luyue, for instance, reported as follows:

> はい、高校の時からずっと、(将来) カントン語を使うとは思っていました。家でも使うし、よく香港には行っているので、日常生活的に便利だと思いました。
>
> [Yes, since high school I thought that I would use Cantonese in the future. I thought the language was useful in my daily life, because I speak it at home and I often visit Hong Kong.]

Only two participants studied English as a second language at high school. One of the participants, Iseok, recognized the possibility of using English in the future while in high school. However, the following statement shows that his motive to learn English was more socially influenced, and thus his future goal for learning the language appeared to be vague:

> I: その当時、英語を将来使うと思っていましたか？
> S はい、英語が必要だとは感じていました。私が英語を学び始めたときも韓国で英語ブームがあって、みんな「英語を学ぼう」と言っているから、英語が大事だと、そんな気持ちがありました。
>
> [I: At that time, did you think you might use English in the future?
> S: Yes, I thought English was necessary. When I started to learn English, Korea was undergoing a boom in learning English and everyone said, 'Let's learn English'. So, I thought English was important.]

Six Australian participants started to learn additional foreign languages (Korean, Mandarin, German and Indonesian) at the university. This is not surprising because the Australian informants do not major in one subject exclusively and have more language options to choose from than the students in the Korean context, where all the informants majored in Japanology. Generally, when choosing an additional language, the Australian participants prefer languages that are linguistically/culturally closer to Japanese, such as Korean and Mandarin. Three informants (Laura, Luyue and Yian) started Korean at the university, while two learners (Laura and Iseok) took courses on Mandarin. Scott and Kris took courses on Indonesian and German, respectively. All six seem to have an interest in language learning in general, as they take these new languages as their third, fourth or fifth language. The motivational relationship between these languages and Japanese will be discussed in the following section.

Relationship between languages: Japanese as a primary language

Domain of L2 self

In order to examine the relationship between different language-specific future self-images within the participants, I adapted the four domains (interpersonal, leisure, career and education) of future self-guide which are utilized in the first Korean study (Table 4.3). Seven learners speak heritage languages, and a number of their comments reflect a self-image of using their heritage languages with their family members, relatives or friends in the future. For instance, Shiyi, who chose to learn Mandarin at the university said, 'I want to be able to speak (Mandarin) more, and specifically communicate because it's my parents' language, and it's a family's language. So, I want to be able to use it, like many other Australian Chinese people here'. As a result, a new subcategory in the interpersonal domain, which implies their future self-image as *family*, emerged naturally from the data.

In addition, the participants had a variety of hobbies that are related to their L2(s) outside of pop culture and travel. For example, Diane (L1: English, L2: French, L3: Japanese) described, 'I think I may use (those three) English, Japanese and French. Because I still play *koto*, and my *koto* teacher speaks Japanese. So, he will talk to us in Japanese. I also do horse riding. A lot of the terms are French. So, I'll still use French a little bit for that'. Consequently, a subcategory entitled *enjoying other interests* also emerged. Overall, a relatively large number of comments in the subcategory of *friends* in the interpersonal domain seem to reflect that many informants have opportunities to communicate with their friends or host families in Japanese. Also, the largest number of comments in the category of *desired job* (career domain) represents the informants' perception to use Japanese in the distant future. Similar to the Korean study, it was sometimes difficult to sort the participants' comments into either domain-specific goals/objects or the related L2 self-guides. As a result, I tried to classify the statements in Table 4.3 according to whether the learner places the emphasis on the cognitive goal or the future vision (for more detailed explanation, see Chapter 3). The numbers in brackets represent learning goals/objects rather than future self-images.

Enhanced interest in L2 learning

One of the most important aspects on the relationship between different languages within the Australian informants is that their interests in Japanese language learning helped arouse interests in learning subsequent second languages. Unlike the Korean context, where English is widely recognized as a privileged L2 (and Japanese as a preliminary L3), Japanese could be a primary L2 for the Australian learners. Especially for the informants in Group 1, it appears that there is no competing powerful language which negatively influences their study of Japanese. In addition, compared with the Korean learners, the Australian learners may have less pressure from graduation requirements and finding employment. In fact, none of them reported that they had suffered pressure in their study of Japanese. These contextual advantages not only help maintain their interests in the target language/culture but also stimulate their interests in learning additional languages. Laura, for example, explained the reasons why she started to study Korean at the university as follows:

> そして最初から言語を勉強するのは楽しくて。その気持ちにも戻りたかったんです。 ... 今は日本人とこのように日本語を話してるのは楽しいですけど、あ・い・う・え・おを学んだ時も楽しかったです。この気持ちもまた（経験したかった）。... ほんとに面白い。最初から学ぶ（こと）の楽しさをまた感じて、日本語の時（を）も思い出して、楽しいです。
>
> [And it is also because I enjoyed learning the language (Japanese) from the beginning, and thus I wanted to get that feeling again ... I enjoy talking with Japanese people in Japanese like this, but I also enjoyed the period when I learnt

Table 4.3 The Australian participants' projected future L2 use

Domains and Subcategories	Jp (n=14)	En (n=2)	Other (n=12)	Hr (n=6)	Examples
Interpersonal					
Friends	11	2	3	3	And I hope that if I can (go) over there (and) make some friends, and have them to communicate with in Japanese. (Emma)
Family				5	Ah, I want to be able to speak more and specifically communicate, because it's my parents' language, and it's a family's language. (Shiyi)
Leisure					
Travelling abroad	3		1	1	私台湾が好きなので、台湾に行く時に苦労しないように(中国語を)勉強したいんです。[Because I like Taiwan, I want to study Mandarin so as to travel to Taiwan without problem.] (Luyue)
Enjoying pop culture	5	1	2	2	レジャーで使うのはだぶんアニメ、マンガとゲームなんで。…日本語で見たい、遊びたいから。 My leisure is anime, manga and game … I want to watch and play them in Japanese. (Luyue)
Enjoying other interests	3	1	1		弓道とか茶道は続けたいですので、それは日本語だけど、 I would like to continue with kyūdō [Japanese archery] and sadō [tea ceremony], for which I will use Japanese. (Laura)
Career					
Desired Job	12	2	5	3(1)	I would really want to work in Japan or work for trading company in Australia as a translator. (Diane)
Education					
Study abroad plan	1				I'll be applying (for exchange) soon … the summer program at A university, maybe. (Dung)
Access to academic resources	0	1			メディアとか他の科目でも、資料を読んで知らない単語がないくらい（英語を）勉強するようにやってます。 I study English to achieve a level where I encounter no unknown words when reading materials for media or other subjects. (Iseok)
Total	35	7	12	14(1)	

*Jp: Japanese/ En: English/ Other (Mandarin, Korean, French, Indonesian, German and Malay)/ Hr: heritage languages (Cantonese, Mandarin, Teochew and Greek).

> a, i, u, e, o [the abc's of Japanese]. I wanted to experience the feeling once again … It's really interesting. Now I find enjoyment in learning a language from the beginning once again and in recalling when I learnt Japanese.]

The words such as 'interesting' and 'enjoyable' reflect that Laura thoroughly enjoyed the process of learning Japanese. It is possible that her strong interest in and desire to experience the process of language learning, which is derived from her learning experience of L2 Japanese, contributed to her decision to study L3 Korean at the university.

Enhanced current L2 self-image

Moreover, the Australian data showed that one's positive experiences learning an L2 not only influences one's interest in the additional languages but also enhances one's current self-image as a language user/learner. This, in turn, positively influences the decision to study an additional language. Laura, for instance, commented as follows:

> （日本語を学んだことによって）自分が言語を勉強することが強いんだとわかって。他のエッセイ書くの、論文書くのは下手だし、あの科学とかも弱いから、これで続こうと思って。韓国語は日本語と似ているし、言語学には興味があるから（韓国語の勉強を始めました）。

> [I found I was good at learning a language [through the study of Japanese]. Since I am poor at other studies, such as writing essays and reports, and science, I decided to continue with language study. [I started to learn Korean,] because the language is close to Japanese and I am interested in linguistics.]

The extract above indicates that through her learning experience of Japanese, Laura developed a positive self-image as an L2 learner, which encouraged her to study a subsequent foreign language. A reverse case came from Emma (L1: English, L2: French, L3: German, L4: Japanese), who noted that her pleasant learning experience with L2 French influenced her decision to study L4 Japanese. When asked about the significant event/people in her learning history of French, she answered that:

> I think probably the major, a sort of, event with it is that through learning French, I sort of, I figured out what I wanted to do with my life. So, through learning French, I knew that I wanted to study languages, study linguistics.

Emma's expression, 'I figured out what I wanted to do with my life', indicates that she came to realize her own capability of learning language through the study of L2 French, which implies the enhancement of her current self-image. The extract above also shows that she envisages herself learning the L2 in the future. In fact, she claims that she can clearly envision herself using Japanese/French in a future career as a language teacher. Therefore, it is conceivable that Emma's French learning experience not only raised her interest in additional languages, but also helped develop her current self-image as an L2 learner, which allowed her to study an additional foreign language.

Cooperative L2 selves

Compared with the Korean data, the Australian data offers more examples which show that the informants' multiple languages are cooperative in constructing their ideal self-images in a particular domain of future life. For instance, consider Laura's description of the relationship between her different languages:

> I: 将来の仕事を考えたとき、どの言語を使うと思いますか?
> S: まあ日本語(の)スキルとして言えば…日本語なら通訳者になれるという事ですが、韓国語と中国語の(今の)レベルだけでは(通訳者には)なれないと思いますので、バックアップとして「私は日本語の通訳者です。そして必要ならば韓国語も中国語もできる」ということで(これらの言語を使うと考えています)。
>
> [I: When you think of your future career, what languages do you think you might use?
> S: Speaking of my Japanese skills… I may become an interpreter. But I think it's difficult to become an interpreter with my current Korean and Mandarin skills. So, I think I'll use these languages as backups, like 'I am a Japanese interpreter, and I can also speak Korean and Mandarin, if needed'.]

The quote above implies that Laura considers L3 Korean and L4 Mandarin as 'backup' languages for L2 Japanese, and that all three languages are synthesized to construct a multilingual vision in the career domain of her future life.

For Iseok (L1: Korean, L2: English, L3: Japanese, L4: Mandarin), Japanese does not seem to be the primary language in his future life, but English is. Japanese was instead chosen as an alternative major by a process of elimination. However, as Iseok's future goal to become a patent lawyer (which is related to English) was constructed, he came to believe that Japanese would also be useful in his future career:

私はむかし法律（の勉強）をはじめてやるとき、やりたかったのは、特許弁護士です。... その仕事は日本のカンパニーとか企業とか会社が、結構多い（特許弁護士の）立場を持っています。だから日本語が使えるなら、自分に有利だと（思うようになりました）。

[When I started to learn law, I wanted to become a patent lawyer ... I came to know that I would have an advantage if I could use Japanese, because lots of Japanese enterprises and companies offer such [patent lawyer] positions.]

Before choosing to major in Japanese at the university, it appeared that Iseok's study of Japanese was merely linked to an interest in pop-culture (leisure domain), and not related to English. However, his career-related ideal self gradually came to include both English and Japanese self-images, although it was still vague. Yian (L1: English, L2: Mandarin, L3: Japanese, L4: Korean), who also started to learn Korean at the university, similarly commented that she envisages her future self-image as a hotel clerk who is able to use four languages interchangeably. This example again indicates that the languages can complement each other to construct a more elaborated multilingual future self-representation especially in the career domain.

In short, in the Australian context, Japanese language learners are more likely to have a positive learning experience than in the Korean context. These experiences help generate and maintain interest in the target language/culture and enhance current self-images as Japanese learners/users. Learners' multiple languages may not always be collaborative in forming ideal self-images, as the learners learn/use different languages for different purposes, in different domains of their life and speak them with different people (Grosjean 2008). Yet, having multiple second languages may at least open up the possibility of developing an elaborated multilingual vision and future self-image in a particular domain (or domains) of life that would not exist in learners of a single L2.

Chapter summary

Many Australian informants were interested in Japanese and Japanese culture, particularly popular culture, from the start of their language learning. Although their cultural/linguistic backgrounds are diverse, their positive L2 learning experiences at high school and in Japan appeared to almost universally translate into commitment to learning Japanese. Similarly, the participants had greater chances to communicate with people in Japanese at university than the Korean participants and most were able to conceive of Japanese as a possible career language. Furthermore, the perceived difficulty of Japanese and effort required to learn seemed to cause some participants to express a desire not to waste the time and energy they had spent on Japanese, creating or reinforcing a feeling that they needed to continue their efforts in order to keep up their language skills. The interview data showed that all of these elements can help evolve learners' initial interests in the language/culture, assist them in setting long-term learning goals and construct their ideal/feared self-images as Japanese users/learners. This is reflected in the general presence of strongly expressed intentions to continue learning Japanese throughout their lives.

5

'I think that English is the first, and the next is Japanese.' Motivational trajectories of Korean learners

Chapters 3 and 4 have provided a baseline picture of their initial motivations and their study experiences and L2 self-perceptions at the time of interview 1. The aim of Chapters 5 and 6 is to conduct a more detailed examination of the learning trajectories of the informants during a seven-month period of their university study. While the course stage varied, at the time of the second interview, all of the participants had moved on in their studies and were thinking in a more focussed way about life beyond their undergraduate course. For this chapter, I will first investigate the changes in the Korean informants' language learning experiences and perceived future use of L2 during the period. I will then describe two (sustained and waning) motivational trajectories detected in analysis of the data. Thereafter, Oyeon and Anbok's cases, which represent the first trajectory, as well as Minseop and Cheonga's cases, which exemplify the second trajectory, will be examined. For the analysis of these motivational trajectories, I will employ the Dynamic Systems Theory (DST).

Language learning experience in seven months

The second interview with the Korean informants was carried out through Skype in May 2015, seven months after the first interview. All the twelve informants participated in the interview, and eight of them preferred to use Japanese (in comparison to four in the first interview), reflecting an increase in the Japanese skills of some participants. As Table 5.1 shows, in the seven-month period, eleven out of twelve informants increased their year level. Pilho, who started his fourth year from the second semester in 2014, progressed to his

Table 5.1 The Korean participants' Japanese-related experiences and changes in perceived competence/confidence in the language

	Year Level	Changes in Major Study	Main Use Outside of the Classroom			Perceived Competence	Perceived Confidence
			Education	Interpersonal	Leisure		
1 Anbok	2		Japanese study club		Study and personal trips; Japanese drama performance	Slightly increased	Slightly increased
2 Junha	2	Started English language and literature				No change	Increased
3 Oyeon	2		Took JPT		Study trip	Increased	(No answer)
4 Nampyo	3					Slightly increased	No change
5 Bosun	3		Took JPT			No change	Decreased
6 Minseop	3	Started economics			Translated Japanese novels; enjoyed pop culture	No change	(No answer)
7 Cheonga	3	Took a year off			Enjoyed pop culture	No change	No change
8 Ihyeong	3		Japanese study club			No change	No change
9 Hongdae	4	Started business administration			Study trip	Slightly decreased	No change
10 Gapsang	4	Took a year off	Japanese study club			No change	No change
11 Daebeon	4				Enjoyed pop culture	Slightly increased	No change
12 Pilho	4	Stopped taking Japanese language class	Took JPT	Communicated with Japanese friends		Slightly decreased	No change

final semester. Two other fourth year students (Hongdae and Pilho) did not take any Japanese language class but took other Japan-related classes (e.g. Japanese politics, Japanese history) offered by the department in the first semester in 2015. Junha, Minseop and Hongdae started to major in another course (English language and literature, economics and business administration, respectively) in addition to Japanology. Cheonga and Gapsang took a year-off from the university at the beginning of the new school year in 2015. These changes in their major and deferrals of their study may indicate their sense of uncertainty about their Japanese study and their future directions. The seven-month period includes the university winter holidays (eight weeks). During the holidays, three informants (Anbok, Oyeon and Hongdae) participated in a short-term exchange programme in a Japanese university for ten days, and Anbok also travelled to Japan privately for another ten days. The participants in general reported that they did not make much effort to study Japanese during this period.

Table 5.1 summarizes the Korean informants' Japanese-related experiences outside of the classroom. Here, their Japanese use experiences outside of the classroom are categorized under the domains of life, which are utilized for the analysis of their projected future L2 use (see Tables 5.2 and 5.3). Importantly, only one participant (Pilho) commented that he used Japanese to communicate with his Japanese friends (interpersonal domain). In the first interview, exposure to Japanese pop culture (leisure domain) played an important role in the Korean informants' decision to study the language at university as well as sustaining engagement in language learning (see Chapter 3). However, as they progressed through their courses, many of them have come to have less time to consume Japanese pop culture (e.g. TV dramas, *anime*). Four of them stated that their perceived communicative competence in the language had increased since the first interview, but two participants reported their decreasing ability.

Examination of the Korean informants' discussion of their language learning experiences in the seven months revealed that many of them were focusing on determining their post-university options. All but one of the Korean informants planned to work immediately after graduation. Some learners reconsidered and changed their future course, while others lost future directions, all of which appeared to exert a significant impact on their motivational trajectories for Japanese. The most noticeable contextual difference between the Korean and the Australian contexts in this respect is the range of options after graduation. Nine out of thirteen Australian learners were interested in taking part in programmes, such as the JET (Japan Exchange and Teaching) Program, and/or entering postgraduate courses, which may enhance their career paths (see Chapter 6).

Table 5.2 Shifts in the Korean participants' projected future L2 use

Domains and subcategories	En 1st	En 2nd	Jp 1st	Jp 2nd	Examples
Interpersonal					
Friends	2	3 (1)	5 (1)	3 (2)	はい。今、日本人の友達がいるので(将来日本語も使います)。 Yes. I will use Japanese as well because now I have Japanese friends. (*Pilho*)
Leisure					
Travelling abroad			1		(日本で)フリーターしながら、稼いだ金で旅行に行きたいっていうことが最終目標になって。 Travelling around Japan with the money that I earn as a part-time worker became my ultimate goal. (*Anbok*)
Enjoying pop culture	3	1	8	3	やっぱり読み物とかアニメ・映画。そういうものを見るときに(日本語を)使うと思います。 I think I will use Japanese when I read books or watch anime and movies. (*Pilho*)
Enjoying other interests		1		2	I think the hobby language will be English. Because, I like playing guitar and piano, and there are many world-famous guitar makers in the USA. (*Junha*)
Career					
Desired Job	7 (1)	6 (2)	8 (1)	6 (4)	I think I will use Korean most for my career, but may use other languages, such as Japanese and English, depending on the circumstances. (*Gapsang*)

Education				
Obtaining academic credentials	(1)	1 (5)	1 (2)	今は、…日本人が受けている日本語検定に挑戦しています。 [I am ... currently attempting the Japanese proficiency test that Japanese people take.] (*Oyeon*)
Study abroad plan		2 (2)	2	こっちの大学と（日本の）A大学と交流する留学システムっていうが機会があって、それをしたいと（思います）。 [There is an exchange system between my university and A University in Japan. I would like to participate in it.] (*Anbok*)
Access to academic resources	1	1	1	I would like to study art theory at a postgraduate school. (*Cheonga*)
Total	13 (1)	11 (3)	26 (9)	19 (8)

Table 5.3 Korean participants' projected future use of Japanese, future learning intentions, and self-evaluation on motivation

	Year Level	Friends 1st	Friends 2nd	Travelling 1st	Travelling 2nd	Pop culture 1st	Pop culture 2nd	Other Interests 1st	Other Interests 2nd	Job 1st	Job 2nd	Study Abroad 1st	Study Abroad 2nd	Academic Credential 1st	Academic Credential 2nd	Academic Resource 1st	Academic Resource 2nd	Future Learning Intentions 1st*	Future Learning Intentions 2nd*	Self-Evaluation on Motivation 2nd**
1 Anbok	2	✓		✓	✓	✓					✓	✓	✓					Forever	Forever	High
2 Junha	2			✓	✓	✓				✓	✓			✓				Until graduation	Until graduation	High
3 Oyeon	2	✓						✓		✓	✓	✓	✓		✓			Forever	Forever	High
4 Nampyo	3	✓				✓		✓		✓	✓	✓			✓			Until graduation	Until achieving fluency	High
5 Bosun	3					✓				✓		✓						Until graduation	Forever	So-so
6 Minseop	3	✓					✓			✓		✓						Until graduation	For some time	Low
7 Cheonga	3	✓				✓				✓		✓		✓	✓		✓	Until graduation	Until graduation	So-so
8 Ihyeong	3	✓	✓			✓	✓				✓	✓						Until graduation	Until graduation	So-so

																		Q1*	Q2*	
9 Hongdae	4									✓			✓	✓				Until graduation	Until graduation	Low
10 Gapsang	4			✓						✓			✓					Until achieving fluency	Until graduation	(No answer)
11 Daebeon	4	✓	✓							✓	✓			✓				Forever	Forever	So-so
12 Pilho	4	✓		✓	✓													Until graduation	Until graduation	So-so
Total		6	5	1	1	8	3	1	2	9	10	4	2	6	3	1	1			

*The participants' answers to the question 'How long do you think you will continue with the study of Japanese?'

**The participants' answers to the question 'How would you rate your motivation for learning Japanese?'

In addition, compared to their Australian counterparts, the Korean university appeared to place more importance on students' job hunting, as each teacher was in charge of counselling students in a particular year level for finding employment. Thus, the Korean informants seemed to experience more external pressure to decide on their career paths while in university than their Australian counterparts did.

Shifts in perceived future use of languages

The first interview revealed that the Korean participants' interests in Japanese language/culture as well as their future self-images in which they use the language are the important factors which influence their commencement and continuation of Japanese language learning. In order to analyze the Korean informants' motivational shifts between the first and second interviews, I first examine the changes in their projected future use of Japanese and that of English. The participants were asked the same questions in both interviews, which include their goals for learning the languages and languages they might use in the future (Appendix 1 and 2). In their responses to these questions, a number of references relating to their perceived future usage of these languages were detected, which are summarized in Tables 5.2 and 5.3.

One of the most noticeable trends shown in these tables is the decline of the total number of references concerning their perceived future usage of Japanese. This change can be seen particularly in *enjoying pop culture* and *obtaining academic credentials*. Although it was not shown in these tables, the concreteness of the participants' future use of Japanese had, in many cases, remained vague since the first interview (see Chapter 3). This is partly reflected in the relatively large numbers in brackets in Table 5.2, meaning learning goals/objects rather than future self-images. While ten informants provided comments on their projected future use of Japanese within the career domain, four of them were classified as goals. These informants did expect that they would use Japanese for future employment, but they had not decided the kind of occupation. Table 5.3 further demonstrates that the Korean participants' future learning intention is not always related to their current motivation to study the language. For example, while Junha's intention to continue with Japanese is relatively weak (he will only continue until graduation), his perceived motivation for study was high. In contrast, Daebeon reported his strong intention to continue the study of Japanese for his whole life, but his perceived motivation for university study was 'so-so'.

However, the number of references for their future use of English has been relatively stable, though the numbers in particular domains, such as *enjoying pop culture*, dropped. It is important to note that Tables 5.2 and 5.3 do not represent the whole picture of the Korean informants' future self-guides. However, the stability and instability in their prospections of future language use shown in the tables may partly be related to the development of their English and Japanese selves. Taking these findings into consideration, the rest of the chapter will investigate dynamic changes in the Korean participants' future self-image and motivation.

Motivational dynamics

For the purpose of identifying dynamic trajectories of the Korean participants' motivation, Dynamic Systems Theory (DST) was utilized as an analytical framework, identifying instances of shifts of dynamic system from one *attractor state* to another, as well as features of *emergence*. The first phase of analysis focused on investigating and comparing the initial motivational states of the twelve participants, changes in the motivational states and self-evaluation on their current motivation for learning the language. As a result, two types of motivational trajectories were detected (Table 5.4). Since DST views dynamic systems as constantly changing, the proposed trajectories can be considered as outcomes of continuous interactions between the system components and interactions with environment (De Bot, Lowie and Verspoor 2007). The next phase of analysis aimed to uncover how various personal and social/environmental factors impacted on the formation of each trajectory through examining a number of individual cases.

Table 5.4 Types of motivational trajectories of the Korean participants

	Defined Trajectories	Pseudonyms
1	Sustained motivational trajectory	*Anbok, Junha, Oyeon, Nampyo*
2	Waning motivational trajectory	*Bosun, Minseop, Cheonga, Ihyeong, Hongdae, Gapsang, Daebeon, Pilho*

First of all, *sustained motivational trajectory* can be described as an upward trend of motivational change, and four participants were categorized into this trajectory. They chose to study Japanese at university largely because of their initial interest in the language/culture. At the university, they started to pay more attention to their future courses and set goals for learning Japanese. These participants constructed their ideal Japanese selves, which were revised upwardly over time in terms of the skills, vividness and the range of domains. All of them reported that their current motivation for learning the language was 'high' (see Table 5.3). Three of them reported that they would continue to study the language 'forever' or 'until being fluent', though Junha expressed his plan to stop the study after graduation.

Eight participants were categorized into the *waning motivational trajectory*. Similar to the first trajectory, they started to learn Japanese mainly because they had a strong interest in the language/culture. They had goals for learning the language after entering university. However, as they progressed in their degrees, some of them came under an institutional pressure to meet graduation requirements, and their ought-to Japanese selves appeared to overshadow their ideal Japanese selves. Also, demands for English as a career language (combined with lack of demand for Japanese) appeared to further contribute to the lack of their long-term Japanese goals/visions. Overall, their ideal Japanese selves appear to have limited motivational power. Indeed, although they still have an interest in the language/culture and intentions to continue the study after graduation, they evaluate their current motivation for learning the language as 'so-so' or 'low' (Table 5.3).

Sustained motivational trajectory

The first type of motivational trajectory can be described as a sustained development of the participants' motivation for learning Japanese through the revision of their ideal Japanese self-image and associated language learning goals. Especially during the period between the two interviews, the students classified into this group invested a lot of time and energy in learning and using Japanese and maintained their interests in the language/culture as well as their perceptions that they would use the language in the future. As they progressed through their university studies, they started to crystallize their future goals. It seems that these learners have revised or constructed more elaborate future images of themselves in which they use Japanese. Among the four participants who are classified in this trajectory, Oyeon and Anbok's cases will be presented below. These informants were chosen because there is a clear contrast between them in terms of their L2 learning experiences and motivational relationship between Japanese and other languages. Both of them were second year students at the time of the second interview and started to learn Japanese mainly because of their wish to obtain the JLPT certificate. However, while Oyeon had a strong interest in the language itself and established a closer relationship with her Japanese friend and thus sustained her enthusiasm to learn the language, Anbok struggled to develop intrinsic goals for learning the language. Also, while Oyeon's ideal Japanese, English and Mandarin selves seemed to coexist within a strong multilingual self-view, Anbok's ideal Japanese self appeared to be developed separately from his ideal English self.

Oyeon's case

When Oyeon was in junior high school, she started to teach Japanese to herself because of her strong desire to obtain higher JLPT scores and to receive praise from others. She described her Japanese learning experiences when in junior high school as follows:

> 日本語を勉強していると、…「えらいね。」と言われて。その賞賛の響き、その賞賛の響きがすごく嬉しくて！…周りの人の視線が好きで。勉強していると、いい意味で目立つよねとか、そういう優越感に浸されていて、…。それで一生懸命勉強したんです。
>
> [When I was studying Japanese … people said 'That's great!'. I was very happy to receive the praises! … I liked to hold the spotlight. When I was studying, I was conscious that I stood out from the crowd (in a good way) and that gave me a sense of superiority … That's why I studied Japanese hard.]

The above extract shows that Oyeon had already established her strong sense of self as a competent Japanese learner through the study of the language. Also, through the engagement, she became more interested in the language itself (e.g. *kanji*), as one of her friends described her as a 'Japanese language lover'. By the time of her graduation from high school, she achieved her goal of obtaining N1, the highest-level certificate of JLPT. Interestingly, however, when entering university, she did not think that she would use Japanese in the future. In the first interview, when asked about the reasons she chose to study the language in university, she answered as follows:

それが、矛盾しているんですけど、…好きで勉強した以外は、(日本語学習の)目標とか確固たる夢がなくて。

[It seems paradoxical, but … I did not have any goals or specific dreams for learning Japanese. I just studied it because I liked it.]

At the time of the first interview, Oyeon already possessed high grades and high results in the JLPT (N1) and JPT (880 out of 990), though she was a first-year student. She also expressed her high confidence in Japanese, '日本語は、自慢話ですけど生活するにはまあ問題ない。自信があります。[In all modesty, I have no problems using Japanese for daily life. I am confident in it.]'. She planned to learn Japanese at a postgraduate school and to pursue a career as a researcher in the field.

Unlike many Korean informants, Oyeon enjoyed learning English when in primary and secondary schools. However, her interest in Japanese gradually came to undermine her study of English, and this tendency was criticized by some people close to her. The following extract from the first interview exemplifies the change in her attitudes towards studying English:

中学生の頃までは英語もものすごく好きで、中学生の頃は日本語よりも英語のほうがすごく上手な子だったんです。…でもいつの間にか逆転して。日本語が本当に好きになったから。

[When in junior high school, I also liked English very much and was much more proficient in English than Japanese … However, it reversed without notice, because I came to like Japanese very much.]

Nonetheless, Oyeon taught herself English while in the university and seemed to envisage herself using the language for her future employment. In the first interview, she compared her perceived future use of English and that of Japanese as follows:

英語は、就職したら少し使う場面では使って。そんなに趣味まではしたくない。…奥の深い英語はあまりやりたくないなって。日本語は奥の深いところまで行きたい。

[I will use English for some situations of my career, but I do not want to study the language as a hobby … I don't want to study English deeply, but want to study Japanese deeply.]

After entering university, Oyeon also started to study Mandarin by herself largely because of her interest in the language itself (i.e. characters, sounds). During the period between the two interviews, she visited a Japanese university for ten days for a short-term exchange. While visiting, she met an exchange student from China but was not able to talk with the student successfully in Mandarin. This experience ignited her passion for communicating not only with Japanese people but also with people around the world. Consequently, she changed her future course from a researcher in Japanese language to an interpreter that requires three languages (English, Japanese and Mandarin). In the second-round interview, she explained the change in her future plan as follows:

> 卒業してからは、最初は、去年は日本語研究者になりたかったんですけど、でも今はちょっと変わったような気がします。... 最近は日本語ばかりだと世界は限られてしまう。そういう現実がわかるようになって。... 今はやりたいことは、通訳？会社の通訳。... 日本語担当の、外国語担当の通訳とか。
>
> [At first, I wanted to become a researcher in Japanese language after graduation, but now my ideas have changed a little bit ... Recently I came to realize that if you study only Japanese, it narrows your horizons ... What I want to become now is an interpreter, an interpreter working for a company ... A Japanese language interpreter, or a foreign languages interpreter.]

As Oyeon's future career goal changed from a researcher to an interpreter, she appeared to start constructing an ideal multilingual self-image in which she uses three languages (English, Japanese and Mandarin) for her employment. Interestingly, in her multilingual vision within the career domain, English seemed to be given higher priority. When asked about languages she might use in the future career, she replied as follows:

> 私は正直に言うと、英語。次が日本語、そして中国語の順番と思っております。
>
> [To be honest, I think that English is the first, and the next is Japanese, and then Mandarin.]

This is because, according to Oyeon, '英語は韓国社会では基本なので (because English is a basic language in Korean society)', and unlike her study of Japanese and Mandarin, her study of English was related almost exclusively to her future employment. This is evidenced by her comment in the second interview:

> 私漢字が大好きで。正直言って中国語の勉強している理由も漢字があるからです。英語も漢字があっ

たら死ぬまでやりたいと思ったかもしれません。...
英語は仕事のための、飯のためって感じなんですけど。... そんなに楽
しくないです。

[I like *kanji* very much. To be honest, the reason why I study Mandarin is also because it has *kanji*. If English had *kanji*, I might think that I want to study it until I die ... I study English for my career, like for a living ... It isn't really fun.]

In spite of the change in her future course, Oyeon attained 940 (out of 990) marks when she resat for the JPT during the period between the two interviews. Also, during the period, she applied for a one-year study abroad programme which is funded by the Japanese government. Here, it appears that she revised her goals for learning Japanese upwardly with the enhancement of her self-confidence in the language. In the second interview, she described her strong sense of self as a competent Japanese learner as follows:

私は（日本語の）専攻を、... 自分のプライドだと思っているので。...
日本語を専攻してないのに日本語が私より上手な人たちを見かけるよ
うになったら、悔しいなと思うようになります。

[I have pride in my major [Japanese] ... So, when I see people who do not major in Japanese, but are better at the language than me, I feel disappointed.]

Oyeon's goals for learning Japanese, or ideal Japanese self, seems to be developed upwardly on the basis of the enhancement of her current Japanese self-image, her continued need for achievement and external recognition.

In DST, *initial conditions* of a complex dynamic system are considered to be influential on the subsequent movement of the system. Initial conditions are defined as 'the state of the various sub-systems at the time one starts measuring' (Verspoor 2015: 38). In the current study, this means identifying the state the motivational system occupied at the time the participants started the study of Japanese. In Oyeon's case, her ideal Japanese self, which was derived from her sense of anticipation to gain academic credential (JLPT), as well as her intrinsic interest in the language, seemed to be initial attractors of her *Japanese motivational system*. As she expressed her wish to attain the full marks of JLPT in the second interview, the initial conditions seemed to exert its impact on the subsequent movement of the system. Further, the initial condition of her Japanese motivational system was also found to be influential on the emergence of a new system, her *Mandarin motivational system*. Oyeon's ideal Japanese self, which was originally connected to the education domain (obtaining academic credentials), appeared to be expanded to the career domain (i.e. a researcher in Japanese) after entering university. Through the travel experiences in Japan, her ideal Japanese self evolved into a more vivid and concrete self-image as an interpreter. Her positive learning and use experiences of Japanese seemed to help enhance her current self-concept as a Japanese learner/user. Partly due to the established current Japanese self and her movement towards achieving it, her ideal Japanese self was revised upwardly. It can also be explained that with the strengthening of the subsystem (i.e. ideal Japanese self), the larger Japanese motivational system was also strengthened.

At university, Oyeon developed a future self-image as a researcher of Japanese language. However, the importance of English as a career language in Korean society and her negative experience that she was not able to communicate successfully with a Chinese university student appeared to contribute to a change in the landscapes of her career-related ideal self-image. In DST terms, her *ideal Japanese self-system* was thrown to a *repeller state*, but then, moved to a new *attractor state*, co-constructing a more cooperative relationship with *ideal English self-system* and *ideal Mandarin self-system*. As a result of the systems' *coadaptation*, a new dynamic system at a higher level, that is, her *ideal multilingual self*, in which she uses the three languages as an interpreter, emerged. In this coadapting process, her ideal English self-system played a central role, reflecting a strong impact of Global English on Korean people's decision making on their future course. In other words, *demands for English as a career language* can be seen as a *system parameter*, which mediates the coadaptation between her L2, L3 and L4 self-systems.

Anbok's case

When Anbok was in the third year of high school, he decided to teach himself Japanese because he received a poor grade in English, which is one of the compulsory subjects for the university entrance examination. He concentrated on the study of Japanese in order to obtain the highest credential (N1) of JLPT, which would be of a great advantage in the exam. Surprisingly, he got the qualification with just a few months of self-study. After he entered the university, however, he lost his goal and thus experienced a decline in motivation for learning Japanese. At the first interview, he clearly said that he did not envision himself using Japanese for his future employment. Anbok also stated that he was seeking an alternative goal for studying the language through positively taking part in various Japanese-related activities at the university, such as Japanese drama performance, and a part-time job. During the seven months, he visited

Japan twice: the first trip was for ten days with his friends, and the second one was a short-term (ten days) exchange programme organized by the university. He enjoyed these trips, and his perceived confidence and communicative competence in Japanese increased as he had various opportunities to communicate with Japanese people. When asked about what he did during the stay in Japan, Anbok replied as follows:

> 鹿児島（にいる）時は学生の家庭のホームステイで。（大学）訪問の時には、鹿児島のもっと奥の田舎っぽく見えるところに行って。その時にはおばあさんとかおじいさんと一緒にホームステイしました。… また、大学生と、… 討論をしました。ある主題をもって討論して発表して。そして（討論）しながら、「ああ、私の日本語もちゃんと通じているな。」って感じて、自信が上がります。

> [When I was in Kagoshima, I stayed with a family of a Japanese student. When I visited the university, I stayed with a grandfather and grandmother in a very rural area … I also participated in discussions with Japanese university students. We discussed particular topics and presented. Through the discussion, I thought like, 'Oh, my Japanese makes sense', and my confidence in Japanese increased.]

Thus, Anbok's perceived future use of Japanese connected to the leisure domain (*travelling abroad*) seemed to become more specific. In the second interview, he explained his new goal for learning the language as follows:

> 今（卒業後に）したいのはアルバイトとか、そんなことをしながら金を稼いで、その後に旅行。やっぱり。今、外国語を学んでいるから、それをちゃんと使える機会を作ろうって（思います）。　…　やっぱり（日本語を学ぶ）最終目標は旅行ですね。

> [What I want to do after graduation is earning money through part-time jobs, and after that, travelling. Since I study a foreign language, I want to have opportunities to use it … My ultimate goal for learning Japanese is travelling.]

Based on Anbok's positive L2 use experiences in Japan and the increase in his perceived confidence and competence in Japanese, his ideal Japanese self which is linked to the leisure domain (*travelling abroad*) seemed to be promoted. In addition, while seeking the alternative goal for learning Japanese, he started to have an interest in the language itself (e.g. Japanese classics). In the second interview, he stated that he wished to continue studying Japanese 'for a lifetime' because of his intrinsic interest in the language, and also reported his 'high' motivation for learning the language.

As for Anbok's study of English, from the outset of the study when in primary school, he was not interested in the language. His motivation for learning the language can rather be characterized as a sense of obligation. In the first interview, when asked if he thought he would use English in the future, Anbok commented as follows:

はい、当時はそう思いました。中学から「英語、英語」と。みんな周りで、「英語、英語、英語、英語」と（言いました）。…ＴＯＥＩＣとか試験がありますよね。あの試験をとってＪＰＴと同じように（仕事の）道具として使うように、…先生とか、親が（言いました）。

[Yes, I thought so at that time. Since when in junior high school, everybody said 'study English, English, English'… There are exams, like TOEIC. Teachers and parents encouraged me to take the exam and make use of it as a tool for employment, just like the JPT.]

Not only Anbok, but some other participants also provided similar comments. Nampyo, for example, explained the importance of English as a career language, 'Since English is a common language, I thought it is always necessary even if you don't have any particular goals … I thought English is needed for my future employment, because it is considered to be compulsory in Korea'.

It seemed that Anbok's perception that he would use English in the future was derived from a social recognition that the language is vital for seeking employment. Despite his perceived low competence and confidence in the language, he also thought that he would continue with English as a career language for a long time. In the second interview, he expressed that he would use English even if he works in Japan, meaning that the language was given a high priority in his future employment. Anbok's ought-to English self appears to play a dominant role in his career-related future self-image.

Within the framework of DST, Anbok's *ideal Japanese self-system*, which is derived from his sense of anticipation to gain academic credential (N1), can be viewed as an attractor which initially exerted a powerful organizing force on his *Japanese motivational system*. Since he concentrated on attaining the credential, the very act of achieving the goal eliminated the sense of anticipation, shifting the system into a *repeller state*, a period of transition when the system moves from one *attractor state* to another. However, through positive travel experiences in Japan, he sought out alternative goals for learning Japanese, which pushed the system into a new state space, where his ideal Japanese self which is linked to travelling abroad is an attractor. One of the most striking things to emerge here is that the initial condition has had an enduring impact on subsequent development of his Japanese motivational system. That is, after losing the initial powerful attractor (ideal self, in which he gains N1), the system seems to have sought out a new attractor state which is also governed by a strong attractor. Anbok's various Japanese learning and use experiences also contribute to the development of his intrinsic interest in Japanese language, which can be viewed as a subsystem of his motivational system. The strengthening of the subsystems (ideal Japanese self, interest in Japanese) contributes to increase the width of attractor basin of his Japanese motivational system. Using the language of DST, Anbok's Japanese motivational system appeared to *self-organize* into a new period of stability and cohesiveness (Larsen-Freeman 2015).

The initial state of Anbok's English motivational system can be characterized as his obligation arisen from a social recognition, or *ought-to English self,* which was relevant to his future employment. The system did not appear to fluctuate considerably over time, which may be partly due to the impact of high *demands for English as a career language* in Korean society, which can be viewed as a *system parameter*. This parameter also appears to have mediated the process of *coadaptation* between his Japanese and English motivational systems. On the one hand, because of the strong parameter, Anbok's English motivational system might be stable over time despite the fluctuation of his coexisting Japanese motivational system. On the other hand, due to the influence of the system parameter, his ideal Japanese self, as a subsystem of the larger Japanese motivational system, might have less opportunity to connect to the career domain of his future life. Therefore, the coadaptation between his English and Japanese motivational systems can be partly influenced by the system parameter.

Waning motivational trajectory

The second type of trajectory can be described as a negative development of the Korean learners' motivation for learning Japanese because of the lack of motivational power of their ideal L2 self. The eight informants' initial motive for learning Japanese was their interest in Japanese (pop) culture. Although they came to expect to use the language for various purposes in the future, such as career and study abroad, their perception of the utility of the language, and its relevance to their future lives appeared to decline. Among the eight participants, Minseop and Cheonga's cases were chosen. This is because they provided useful comments, which enabled the researcher to understand how different social and experiential factors influenced the development of their motivation for learning Japanese.

Minseop's case

A third-year student, Minseop, started to have an interest in Japanese language when in junior high school because of his interest in Japanese *anime* and TV drama. Also, when in high school, he learnt the language through communicating with a Japanese friend who was a member of Minseop's basketball club. However, despite his interest in Japanese culture and his usage of the language, the language was not directly related to his future life, as he claimed, 'I did not think that I would use Japanese in the future and major in Japanology'. Minseop explained that his interest in Japanese pop culture seemed to be a chief reason to choose to learn the language at university. At the time of the first interview, he had been introduced to an IT-related job, which requires Japanese proficiency, from a graduate. This helped him envision himself using the language in the work place. In the interview, he commented, 'Because I have heard so much about it [IT-related employment] recently, I would like to pursue it'. After a while, however, the graduate resigned from the job for some reasons. As a result, Minseop started to reconsider about his future course. His prospect of using Japanese for his future career had become unclear. In the second interview, he also said as follows:

> I: In the last interview, you said that you would talk with your friends in Japanese, if you get the IT job and work in Japan, didn't you? ... Don't you imagine yourself working in Japan, now?
> S: It's not clear.

The interview extract above indicates that Minseop's perceived future utility of Japanese, which was linked to a Japanese-related job and to 'friends', has also become less clear. Further, as he started double majors (Japanology and economics) in the new semester, his teacher recommended him to focus more on the study of economics than Japanese. This is because his JPT score approximated to the point required for graduation (670 out of 700). The following quote describes how his teacher is influential in directing and constraining his study of Japanese:

> Because my teacher said, 'Your Japanese is good enough. So, study economics'. The teacher said that it is OK if I possess just enough marks of Japanese proficiency test for graduation.

As Minseop came to concentrate on the study of economics, his motivation for learning Japanese seemed to decline. In the second interview, he described his motivation for learning Japanese as 'low' and commented, 'To be honest, I will not study Japanese at university … unless I need it to get the required marks in the JPT'. Despite the decline in his current motivation for learning Japanese at university, Minseop expressed his intention to continue engaging with the language for a long time, which was largely due to his interest in pop culture. When asked about languages he might use for his future leisure activities, he answered, 'I think I will use Japanese for reading literature or watching *anime* and movies and things like that', which indicates that his ideal Japanese self is linked to the leisure domain.

In contrast to his study of Japanese, Minseop initially had little interest in learning English, which he studied from the third year of primary school to the first semester of university. Nonetheless, he thought he might use the language in his future employment. The following two quotes describe his study of English when in high school:

> I studied English not because I was interested in it, but because I wanted a good grade.
>
> I studied it because a high school teacher said that English is necessary for finding employment and also after getting employment.

These extracts show that Minseop's initial motive for learning English was strongly related to academic goals and his future employment. After entering university, he still seemed to perceive a particular importance of English for his career paths. In the first interview, he claimed that no matter what career he might pursue, he will use English for the career. However, he also said that 'I think I will not use English except for job'. In the second interview, he reiterated that 'I think I will use English only when joining a company'. That is to say, his motivation for learning English has been strongly linked to his future career but very little related to interest and other (e.g. leisure, interpersonal) domains of future life.

From a perspective of DST, Minseop's *Japanese motivational system* was initially in an *attractor state* where his interest in Japanese pop culture and ideal Japanese self linked to the leisure domain were important attractors. As he started to envision an ideal self-image in which he works for an IT-related company, his *ideal Japanese self-system* might be strengthened, which allowed the larger Japanese motivational system to move into a new attractor state. During the period between the two interviews, however, his career-related ideal Japanese self appeared to become vague. This is probably because of the commencement of another major (economics), a loss of future direction related to his friend's experiences and a generally negative impression of the usefulness of Japanese for his career. As he reported his decreasing motivation, the larger Japanese motivational system might weaken, partly due to the weakening of the subsystem (ideal Japanese self-system). Minseop's Japanese motivational system seemed to move into a state space where his interest in Japanese pop culture and ideal L2 self connected to the leisure and education (i.e. JPT) domains are the attractors.

With respect to Minseop's *English motivational system*, the initial conditions also seem to have exerted a significant impact on the subsequent development of the system. That is, his ought-to English self, which can be seen as an initial attractor, or subsystem, has been at the heart of the larger English motivational system. It seems that his *ought-to English self-system* has been lodged in a deep attractor state over time, and similar to Anbok's case, *demands for English as a career language* plays a role of a system parameter. Mercer (2015) suggests that the degree of a system's stability is influenced by the range of the system parameters. That is, when a system has a broad range of parameters, the system is more likely to be shifted by the change of the parameters. As Minseop's English has been almost exclusively related to his future career over time, it is possible that the relative stability of his English motivational system is maintained not only by the strength of the parameter (demands for English as a career language) but also by the limited range of the parameters.

Cheonga's case

Another informant who represents the waning motivational trajectory is a third-year student, Cheonga. In her case, the decline in her motivation was partly related to the institutional requirement to obtain academic credentials, which she perceived difficult to achieve. When she was a second-year high school student, she commenced formal study of Japanese. Her initial motive to learn the language was her interest in Japanese TV programmes and *anime*. As Cheonga became interested in art, her study of Japanese came to be linked to studying art in the future. After entering university, she came to perceive future utility of the language in other life domains. That is, in the first interview, she expressed that she would use the language for studying abroad, communicating with friends and enjoying pop culture (Table 5.3). However, at the same time, her enthusiasm for learning Japanese gradually decreased because of the extrinsic goals to attain required JPT/JLPT scores, which can be interpreted as her ought-to Japanese self. In the first interview, she commented that she was in a struggle between her personal wish to enjoy learning Japanese and the external goal set by the university (see Chapter 3). Also, in the second interview, Cheonga evaluated her motivation for learning Japanese as 'so-so' and explained the reason for the motivational decline as follows:

> I guess it is because of Japanese proficiency test. I expected that studying for the proficiency test would increase my motivation for learning Japanese, but it rather dampened my motivation because of the difficulty.

Cheonga's motivational decline seems to be related to both the necessity to prioritize academic goals at the expense of the intrinsic goals with which she started the study and her perception that the academic goals were going to be very difficult to achieve.

During the period between the first and second interviews, Cheonga decided to take a year off from the university mainly because of her wish to have a break and to travel. Her decision was also influenced by her three friends who were also taking a year off and said, 'You had better take a year off and do what you want to do before graduation'. Another informant, Gapsang, also took a year off from the university in order to escape from the stress of study, as well as to engage in what he was interested in (designing clothing). This intermission, however, does not mean a total suspension of study of Japanese, as these participants learned the language by themselves during the period. Nonetheless, in the second interview, Cheonga's perception to use Japanese in the future seemed to become less clear. She explained in the second interview as follows:

> I: Last year, when I asked about your goals for learning Japanese ... you said that you want to go to Japan as an exchange student, didn't you? How about this goal?
> S: I don't think about the goal at this moment, because I am taking time off. I want to think again, after I return to university.

The interview extract above shows how the change of environment (taking a year off) restricted the construction of Cheonga's ideal Japanese self, which is associated with study abroad, but she still imagined herself using the language for her future career (art-related enterprise). In the interview, when asked about the languages she might use in her future career, she answered, 'I think it's either English or Japanese'.

Cheonga studied English from the third year of primary school to the first year of university. While her study of English was largely influenced by social value (see Chapter 3), she also had a personal interest in consuming English pop culture (TV dramas). As she came to dream of art-related career paths, she started to perceive future utility of English which is connected to studying art. In the first interview, she stated, 'Because I wanted to study art, I thought learning many languages would be beneficial for my study of art'.

In the university, although Cheonga did not study English formally, she appeared to envision herself using the language in a number of domains of her future life (e.g. enjoying pop culture, desired job). In the first interview, when asked about languages she might use in her future leisure activities, she stated, 'I think both Japanese and English will be useful for my future hobby ... For example, when I watch TV dramas and meet friends'. However, in the second-round interview, Cheonga answered to the same question, 'Because my hobby is indoor activity, I don't think I will use Japanese and English for that'. Thus, Cheonga's one-year off from the university seemed to negatively affect not only her projection to use Japanese but also that of English.

In DST terms, Cheonga's interest in Japanese pop culture as well as her ideal Japanese self-image relating to art can be seen as initial attractors, or subsystems, of her *Japanese motivational system*. However, as she progressed through her university study, her ought-to Japanese self, which was derived from the institutional pressure to obtain academic credentials, appeared to be activated. In addition, in the first interview, her ideal Japanese self was linked to various domains of her future life. This means that the attractor basin of her *ideal Japanese self-system* was wide, and thus, the system had a more varied range of conditions that can easily drive the system toward the *attractor state* (Hiver 2015). However, due to the difficulties in Japanese study and her move out of the educational system, her ideal Japanese self, which was linked to the leisure, education and interpersonal domains, seemed to become less activated. With the weakening of the subsystem (ideal Japanese self-system), Cheonga's Japanese motivational system might also be weakened, or pushed to a *repeller state*.

The initial conditions of Cheonga's *English motivational system* also seemed to be characterized as her interest in enjoying English TV dramas as well as her ideal English self, in which she studies art. Similar to her Japanese motivational system, after she took a year off, her interest in English pop culture appeared to decrease, whereas her perception to use English for her future career was relatively stable, which means that her career-related ideal English self played a significant role in stabilizing her English motivational system. Although both her study of Japanese and that of English are linked to her art-related future employment, Cheonga did not provide any comments which indicate either the competition between her ideal Japanese and English selves or the construction of her multilingual vision. Rather, her ideal Japanese and English self-systems appear to have little to do with each other, which is in marked contrast to Oyeon's case.

Chapter summary

This chapter revealed a number of important aspects of the Korean participants' motivational development over the seven-month period. First of all, initial motivational states, which were identified in the first Korean study, have a significant impact on the subsequent development of their motivation. The participants' initial interest in and liking for Japanese language/culture tended to be maintained, even where additional motivations were added to this base. As Anbok's case indicated, if one's L2 motivational system, which was initially lodged in a deep attractor state is thrown into an unstable state, the system tends to return back to a deep attractor state, which is similar to the initial state. In contrast, as Cheonga's case showed, when the initial motivator could not be pursued, due to more important external goals, motivation as a whole declined. Secondly, the development of the participants' ideal Japanese self related to the career domain significantly affect their motivation for learning Japanese. More precisely, as they progress their university study, whether or not they are able to construct or evolve their ideal Japanese self-image, which is especially linked to the career domain, seems to be one of the most important factors which can determine their motivational trajectory. Here, whether the participants are successful in Japanese study is closely related to the construction/revision of their ideal Japanese selves. Indeed, those informants who are classified in sustained motivational trajectory were all succeeding in achieving their academic and other goals, which appeared to facilitate the upward revision of their ideal L2 selves. In contrast, the participants who are classified under waning trajectory were not successful in their study. Minseop's goals for learning Japanese did not continue to expand, and Cheonga was not able to reach necessary academic goals. Their unsuccessful learning experiences appeared to be related to their declining motivation. Finally, the coadaptation between their Japanese and English motivational systems was often mediated by a system parameter, *demands for English as a career language*. In Oyeon's case, by the influence of the system parameter, her coexisting ideal Japanese, English and Mandarin self-systems started constructing her ideal multilingual self-system in which English plays a central role. As Henry (2015) points out, system parameters do not control the whole trajectory of the system's movement by themselves, rather, it is the system's own dynamics, or *self-organization*, which determines the system's behaviour. In this sense, the system parameter, demands for English as a career language, may mediate the self-organization of, or coadaptation between, the Korean informants' Japanese and English motivational systems.

It should be noted that, however, there is also a case which indicates a contrastive relationship between the participant's Japanese and English motivational systems. A third-year student, Nampyo's future goal for learning English became less clear after entering university. Although he initially stated that he would study English in order to attain a desired TOEIC score, in the second interview he claimed, 'At this moment, I do not intend to study English at all'. According to him, this is because of the competition among the students. In other words, he has invested his energy more in improving Japanese proficiency in order to distinguish himself from other students. This has contributed to the decrease in his perceived future utility in English, and thus, the weakening of his English motivational system. Taken together, there seem to be three types of coadaptation between ideal L2 and L3 self-systems. First, the two systems within a learner can grow together and consolidate into a stronger ideal multilingual-self system, and the learner can keep expanding competence in both (e.g. Oyeon's case). Second, when one system is weakened, it can trigger the weakening of the other system. Third, as Nampyo's case showed, when one system is weakened, it can result in the strengthening of the other system (see also Henry 2017). Although Cheonga's case did not provide clear evidence which indicates interaction between her Japanese and English motivational systems, this can still be classified in one of the three types, because DST supposes that coexisting dynamic systems are inextricably related to each other.

Having discussed that, a question arises as to what extent the Korean Japanese language learners' motivational trajectories, including the systems' initial conditions, the development of the subsystems (e.g. ideal Japanese self-system), coadaptation with other motivational systems and the system parameters, are applicable to other contexts. The next chapter will, thus, focus on the motivational trajectories of the Australian participants.

6

'I really, really want to do Japanese translating.' Motivational trajectories of Australian learners

This chapter focuses on the trajectories of the Australian participants' motivation for learning Japanese during the period between the first and second interviews. It first examines general trends in their language learning experiences and significant changes in their expectations about future language use during the period and identifies two types of motivational trajectories. Afterwards, four participants' (Emma, Laura, Scott and Iseok) cases are investigated in relation to these trajectories in order to further illuminate the dynamics of L2 selves and motivation.

Language learning experience in seven months

All but one of the Australian informants (Debra) participated in the second interview, which was conducted in October 2015. While four of the fourteen initial participants spoke in Japanese in the first interview, six preferred to use Japanese for the second round. The seven-month period between the first and second interviews almost covered a whole university school year. Scott, Emma and Xin had entered their final year of university. In the second semester, one informant (Scott) did not take Japanese classes, but the rest of the informants took at least one Japanese class throughout the 2015 university year. Table 6.1 summarizes the Australian informants' Japanese-related experiences in and outside of the classroom. Importantly, the Australian informants had more chances to use/speak Japanese in and outside of the classroom (for instance, at the Japanese club in university or during a business Japanese unit) than their Korean counterparts over the same period. The table also shows that six learners'

Table 6.1 The Australian participants' Japanese-related experiences and changes in perceived competence/confidence in the language

	Year Level	Studying Japanese as a...	Japanese Course	Main Use Outside of the Classroom				Perceived Competence	Perceived Confidence
				Education	Career	Interpersonal	Leisure		
1 Laura	2	Major	Advanced Professional	Interviewed a businessman	Volunteered as an interpreter			Slightly increased	Increased
2 Diane	2	Major	Proficient			Communicated with exchange students and host mother		Slightly decreased	No change
3 Scott	3	Minor	Proficient			Communicated with a Japanese friend and a high school teacher		Slightly decreased	No change
4 George	2	Major	Proficient		Talked with customers	Taught Japanese to his colleagues		Increased	Increased
5 Emma	4	Major	Proficient			Communicated with Japanese friends		Slightly increased	Increased
6 Luyue	3	Major	Advanced Professional	Interviewed a businessman			Played video games	Slightly increased	Decreased
7 Shiyi	1	Major	Advanced			Communicated with Japanese friends		Increased	No change

8 Jiajie	2	Major	Proficient		Communicated with a Japanese girlfriend and exchange students	No change	No change
9 Yian	2	Major	Proficient		Communicated with an Australian friend	No change	No change
10 Xin	3	Minor	Proficient		Exchanged email with a Japanese friend	No change	Decreased
11 Iseok	3	Major	Advanced Professional	Interviewed a businessman		No change	Slightly decreased
12 Kris	2	Major	Proficient		Communicated with Japanese friends	No change	Slightly increased
13 Dung	2	Major	Proficient		Communicated with exchange students	Increased	No change

perceived competence in Japanese had improved since the first interview, and four informants' self-confidence in the language had increased.

Similar to the Korean context, the Australian participants' growing focus on determining their post-university options seemed to have a considerable impact on their motivational shifts. However, compared with their Korean counterparts, the Australian informants showed a more consistent trend towards crystallizing their future studies or careers. As for changes in the participants' future plan to study Japanese, while none clearly stated that they would study Japanese at a postgraduate level in the first interview, six out of thirteen had decided to take a master's course in Japanese by the second round. Five participants (Laura, Diane, Emma, Luyue and Dung), who were all aiming to become translators or interpreters, had begun planning to take a double master's in translating and interpreting. This is a two-year course established at their university in collaboration with a Japanese university, in which students complete the first year in Australia and the second year in Japan. Kris also stated his intention to take a general master's in translating and interpreting in either Australia or Japan. Since four out of the six informants are the second-year students who decided to major in Japanese, it is possible that this decision to officially major influenced their future plans to study the language. In addition, three participants (Laura, Emma and Dung) stated that they were going to apply for the Japan Exchange and Teaching (JET) Programme before starting the double master's course. The JET Programme is a Japanese government-sponsored programme in which participants are employed, for instance, as an assistant English teacher in Japan (Japan Exchange and Teaching Programme 2017). These emerging plans for further vocational-focused study or short-term employment in Japan appeared to be influential in the development of projected future use of Japanese in the education and career domains.

Shift in perceived future use of languages

For the purpose of examining the motivational dynamics of the Australian participants, I first investigated changes in their projected future usage of languages in terms of domains of possible selves. Similar to the Korean study, the Australian participants were asked the same questions about their goals and future plans for their language learning in the first and second interviews (Appendices 1 and 2). References relating to their future use of languages made in their responses to these questions were categorized in terms of domain of future life and are summarized in Tables 6.2 and 6.3.

Table 6.2 Shifts in the Australian participants' projected future L2 use

Domains and subcategories	Jp (n=13)		En (n=2)		Other (n=12)		Hr (n=6)		Examples
	1st	2nd	1st	2nd	1st	2nd	1st	2nd	
Interpersonal									
Friends	11	11	2	2	3	6	3	2	And I definitely want to go back over to Japan, visiting my family and friends again. (*Diane*)
Family						2	5	5	To my parents, it will be Chinese and English. (*Yian*)
Leisure									
Travelling abroad	3	2			1	1	1		I hope to travel a lot and live in both areas (Japan and Indonesia) and try to improve my language a lot. (*Scott*)
Enjoying pop culture	5	7	1		2	4	2	1	趣味といえば、私はアニメやゲームやマンガしかないので、（趣味で使う言語は）たぶん70パーセント日本語です。[Since my hobby is limited to anime, game and manga, my hobby language will be Japanese for 70 per cent.] (*Luyue*)
Enjoying other interests	3	5	1	1	1	3			(将来) 小説を書く時は、たいてい最初に日本語を書いて、後で英語に翻訳します。[When I write a novel in the future, I will write it in Japanese at first, and then, translate it in English later.] (*George*)
Career									
Desired job	12	11	2	2	5	4	4	2	I really want to try to get a job [at the] Japan Olympics ... So, if I can be like a translator or something for one of the teams. (*Scott*)
Education									
Study abroad plan	1	6							And then I want to come back and get a master's in translation and interpretation at A University with B University (in Japan). (*Emma*)
Access to academic resources			1						メディアとか他の科目でも資料を読んで知らない単語がないくらい(英語の)勉強するようにやっています。[I study English hard so that I can read papers on media and other subjects without any unknown words.] (*Iseok*)
Total	35	42	7	5	12	20	15	10	

*Jp: Japanese/ En: English/ Other (Mandarin, Korean, French, Indonesian, German and Malay)/ Hr: heritage languages (Cantonese, Mandarin, Teochew and Greek).

Table 6.3 Australian participants' projected future use of Japanese, future learning intentions, and self-evaluation on motivation

	Year Level	Studying Japanese as a…	Friends 1st	Friends 2nd	Travelling 1st	Travelling 2nd	Pop culture 1st	Pop culture 2nd	Other Interests 1st	Other Interests 2nd	Job 1st	Job 2nd	Study Abroad 1st	Study Abroad 2nd	Future Learning Intentions 1st	Future Learning Intentions 2nd	Self-Evaluation on Motivation 2nd
1 Laura	2	Major	✓							✓	✓	✓		✓	Until graduation	Forever	High
2 Diane	2	Major	✓	✓		✓			✓	✓	✓	✓			Forever	Forever	High
3 George	2	Major	✓	✓						✓	✓	✓			Until achieving fluency	Until achieving fluency	High
4 Emma	4	Major	✓	✓			✓	✓							Forever	Forever	High
5 Luyue	3	Major	✓	✓			✓	✓			✓	✓		✓	Until graduation	Until achieving fluency	High
6 Jiajie	2	Major	✓	✓				✓			✓	✓		✓	Forever	Forever	High
7 Kris	2	Major	✓	✓			✓				✓	✓		✓	Forever	Until achieving fluency	High
8 Dung	2	Major		✓				✓			✓	✓		✓	Forever	Forever	High
9 Yian	2	Major	✓								✓	✓			Until achieving fluency	Until achieving fluency	High
10 Xin	3	Minor					✓	✓		✓	✓	✓			Until graduation	Until graduation	High
12 Scott	3	Minor	✓	✓	✓		✓		✓	✓	✓	✓			Forever	Forever	So-so
13 Shiyi	1	Major	✓	✓	✓		✓	✓			✓				Forever	Forever	So-so
11 Iseok	3	Major	✓	✓	✓			✓		✓	✓	✓			Forever	Forever	So-so
Total			11	11	3	2	5	7	3	5	12	11	1	6			

Through the analysis of the participants' statements concerning their perceived future use of languages and comparison of these replies with those of the Korean participants, a number of trends were identified. First of all, the total number of domain-related references increased from the first interview, particularly for *study abroad plan*. Second, the Australian participants appeared to possess more stable ideal Japanese selves than their Korean counterparts. While the Korean learners showed a tendency to lose interest in Japanese pop culture, the number of Australian learners in *enjoying pop culture* remained steady. The more stable number in *friends* may reflect the fact that the Australian informants had more steady relationships with Japanese friends or host families compared with the Korean informants. Third, although it cannot be shown in these tables, the concreteness of the Australian learners' perceived use of Japanese in the future, in general, also seemed to increase in the seven-month period. Finally, the total number of references of the Australian participants' future use of *other* languages increased, whereas those of *English* and *heritage* languages slightly declined overall. As was mentioned in Chapter 5, the table does not represent a full view of the informants' future self-guides. Nevertheless, the changes and stability in the Australian informants' projections of future language use shown in the table may partly reflect the characteristics of their language-specific self-images and motivational trajectories.

Table 6.3 shows the Australian informants' statements regarding their intentions for Japanese study after graduation. Eight out of thirteen participants said that they would study Japanese forever, or for a lifetime, in both the first and second interviews. The first Australian study concluded that their strong interest in Japanese language/culture and elaborated self-images as Japanese users/learners seem to play a vital role in the general presence of their strong intentions to continue lifetime learning of Japanese (see Chapter 4). However, Table 6.3 further demonstrates that the participants' future learning intention is not always linked to their current motivation to study Japanese. For instance, although Scott, Shiyi and Iseok reported that they would sustain studying Japanese, they described their current motivation for learning the language as 'so-so'. In contrast, while Xin's (L1: English, L2: Mandarin, L3: Malay, L4: Japanese) intention for continuing Japanese study can be classified as relatively weak, her perceived motivation for current academic study of Japanese was 'high'. This tendency is identical to the Korean context (Chapter 5).

Motivational dynamics

Drawing on a similar procedure to the second Korean study (Chapter 5), I investigated the Australian participants' initial motivational states, changes in their motivational states and self-evaluation on their current motivation through the use of two face-to-face interviews. Similar to their Korean counterparts, the Australian participants were also classified under the two identified types of motivational trajectories, as seen in Table 6.4.

First of all, *sustained motivational trajectory* represents an upward development of motivation. Ten of the thirteen Australian informants (Laura, Diane, George, Emma, Luyue, Jiajie, Kris, Dung, Yian and Xin) were classified under this category. All ten initially had an interest in Japanese language and culture, and nine reported in the second interview that they had maintained their interest. Their study of the language was often facilitated by their pleasant experiences in high school and Japan. They provided more positive and intrinsic motives to choose to study the language at university than their Korean counterparts (see Chapter 5). At the university, they started to pay more attention to their future, and their desires to pursue careers relating to Japanese (such as translator, engineer) appeared to become stronger.

The second interview also revealed that through various Japanese learning/use experiences, such as participating in the Japanese club, or taking a business Japanese course, some informants' perceived competence and/or confidence in Japanese improved (see Table 6.1). This means that their current self-views as Japanese users had enhanced. Their continued establishment of relationships with Japanese friends and the enhancement in their perceived competence/confidence in Japanese seemed to help boost their expectations of using the language in the future. For instance, Dung (L1: Vietnamese, L2: English, L3: Japanese), a second-year student, joined a Japanese club between the two interviews. This granted her opportunities to communicate with Japanese exchange students and club members in Japanese:

Table 6.4 Types of motivational trajectories of the Australian participants

	Defined Trajectories	Pseudonyms
1	Sustained motivational trajectory	*Laura, Diane, George, Emma, Luyue, Jiajie, Kris, Dung, Yian, Xin*
2	Waning motivational trajectory	*Scott, Shiyi, Iseok*

日本のクラブ、Jiajieのクラブ、一緒に行って、留学生たちと話
して、それで私の砕けた話し方は良くなった。... そして一緒に
出かけたりとか、いろいろな日本の文化とか教えてもらって。...
だから、もっと（日本に）行きたいと（思うように）になった。

[Since I joined the Japanese club, Jiajie's [Participant 6] club, and talked with students from Japan, my informal Japanese speech has gotten better ... We went out together, and I was taught about things like Japanese culture ... That's why I now want to go to Japan even more.]

Dung also reported that she applied for an exchange (Australia–Japan) programme offered by her university, just prior to the second-round interview. Due to the enhancement of the informants' current L2 selves, their ideal L2 selves appeared to have been updated, or evolved, in terms of vividness and elaborateness over the seven-month period. Further, six of the ten informants (Laura, Diane, Emma, Luyue, Kris and Dung) started to consider beginning a master's degree which required study in Japan and Australia. Three of them (Laura, Emma and Dung) also set another goal of participating in the JET Programme before taking the master's course. It seemed that the establishment of these subsidiary goals helped them crystallize their ultimate career goals, or at least the steps required to achieve them.

All the informants evaluated their current motivation for learning the language as 'high', and nine of them expressed their strong intentions to continue to study the language 'forever', or until becoming fluent enough (Table 6.3). If we look at this trajectory from a DST perspective, the participants' *interest in Japanese language/culture* and their *ideal Japanese self* can be conceived of as subsystems of the larger *Japanese motivational system*. Because of the development of these subsystems, the larger motivational system increased the width and depth of the *attractor basin*, and thus, achieved a greater stability.

In contrast, three participants (Iseok, Scott and Shiyi) were categorized under the *waning motivational trajectory*. Their motivation for learning Japanese showed a relative decline between the interviews. Similar to the other participants, these three were initially interested in Japanese language or culture and came to envisage their ideal self-image as Japanese users as they accumulated Japanese-related experiences. However, compared with the first type of trajectory, in which the ideal and current Japanese self-images interact with each other and develop along with increasing foci towards future employment, the second type centres the participants' needs outside of career. In other words, three participants stopped imagining further extensions of their ideal Japanese selves because they already achieved their leisure-related ideal Japanese selves (e.g. travelling abroad, enjoying pop culture) or had difficulties in studying Japanese. For instance, Shiyi (L1: English, L2: Mandarin, L3: French, L4: Indonesian, L5: Japanese), a first-year student, had been interested in Japanese pop culture, but her future career goal was vague. As she was strongly recommended by surrounding people (e.g. family members, teachers and friends) to pursue a career in law over Japanese-related employment, her perceived utility of the language for her future career seemed to decline.

All three of the second group of informants expressed decreasing enthusiasm for learning Japanese. Although they thought they might be able to use Japanese in a number of domains of their future life and had intentions to keep studying the language 'forever' (see Table 6.3), they evaluated their current motivation for learning the language as 'so-so' in the second interview. That is, although they did or could envision future self-images in which they use Japanese, their ideal Japanese self came to have less motivational power than before as their future self-guide became vague or the gap between it and their current Japanese self diminished. Considering this trajectory in terms of DST, we can say that the weakening of the informants' ideal Japanese self-system contributed to a decrease in the depth of their larger Japanese motivational system.

Sustained motivational trajectory

Sustained motivational trajectory can be described as a continuing development of the participants' ideal L2 self through the interaction with other motivational factors, such as L2 learning experiences and the current L2 self. Among the ten participants who are classified in this trajectory, Emma and Laura's cases will be discussed below as representatives of the general trends and findings. These two informants were chosen partly because they had quite different learning experiences and proficiency in Japanese. While Emma started her formal study of Japanese after entering university and was taking the proficient level course, Laura had studied the language for a total of five years at secondary school and in Japan prior to the commencement of her study at university and was taking a post-advanced course. Also, the two cases show a clear contrast in the relationship between their motivation for learning Japanese and that for other languages. Emma's increased projection of future use of Japanese was in stark contrast to her projections of French, whereas Laura's perceived future utility of

L2 Japanese seemed to positively influence her expectation for using L3 Korean and L4 Mandarin in the future.

Emma's case

When the first interview took place, Emma (L1: English, L2: French, L3: German, L4: Japanese) was a fourth-year student who had only one year left in university. She was brought up in an Australian family who speaks only English. After graduating from high school, she got a job and started to learn French at a local community centre. Emma's initial reason to commence studying French was not very clear, as she indicates, 'I needed something to do because I was bored with just working. So, I needed something engaging'. However, as her study of French progressed, Emma came to have a strong interest in French culture (particularly films and novels). She expressed that she became aware of her 'saving grace' of being good at learning foreign languages. Her enhanced self-confidence in French, which can be viewed as a part of her current French self-concept, appeared to arouse her enthusiasm for learning the language.

Emma's enhanced self-confidence in French also seemed to trigger her interest in learning additional languages. As referred to in Chapter 4, she decided to major in linguistics as well as Japanese at the university. She chose L4 Japanese due to a curiosity towards the language which arose from its linguistic distance from her first (English), second (French) and third (German) languages. In addition, she believed that native speakers of English have more advantages in finding employment in Japan, which further reinforced her decision to study Japanese instead of French. The following statement from the first interview shows that she anticipated working in Japan as an English teacher:

> I'm still interested in teaching, I really want to teach languages ... I thought the best opportunity to do that ... French or Japanese, probably be Japanese, because I know that they want native English speakers to go there and teach [English]. So, I figured that majoring in Japanese, continuing Japanese, the one I was more interested in than French.

Additionally, just before entering the university, Emma travelled around Japan for one month. As seen in the following quote from the first interview, this appeared to have a considerable impact on her subsequent study of the language:

> S: I guess in terms of, definitely, in terms of my motivation, before it was, sort of, just something that I had to do, because I had to do two

languages. So, it was more of an obligation. But, after going there ... it definitely, sort of, changed my entire focus towards the language.
I: Do you want to visit Japan again?
S: Yes, I really want to go over there next year ... I am going to apply for the JET Programme at the end of this year.

Emma's positive experiences in Japan triggered her interest in Japanese language/culture and also helped her construct a future self-representation that is linked to the career domain.

During the seven-month period between interviews, Emma joined the committee of the Japanese club, which is one of the largest student clubs at her university. She also started to learn Japanese through a mobile application which enabled her to communicate with native speakers of Japanese at any time. As a result, she came to have many more opportunities to communicate with people in Japanese than before. In the second interview, she reported that these experiences helped increase her perceived competence and confidence in the language and boosted her motivation for using/learning Japanese.

At the same time, Emma searched out her 'dream job' as a translator of foreign films working for a TV station and came to be interested in a double master's in translation and interpretation which was introduced by the university. Consequently, she changed her future career goal from a language teacher to a translator and decided to take the master's course after participating in the JET Programme. In the second interview, she explained as follows:

I'm in the middle of my application for JET Programme. I'm applying now ... And then I want to come back and get a master's in translation and interpretation at A University with B University [in Japan] ... But, you have to pass, you have to go in front of the panel and be able to speak fluent Japanese to get into, which I can't do. So, I'm hoping after a few years of living over there [through the JET Programme] ... I can communicate very fluently, and then come back and do that [the master's programme].

Emma's earlier chief aim for participating in the JET Programme, gathering an experience as an English teacher, was shifted to preparation for entering the master's course. The setting of two successive goals (JET Programme and a master's degree) appeared to make her ultimate goal of becoming a translator feel more attainable and also allowed her to develop more options for her future career.

As for the relationship between Emma's two languages (L2 French and L4 Japanese), her perception for future usage of Japanese seems to have gradually exceeded that for French over time. In the first interview, when asked about languages she might use for her future career, she replied 'Japanese, and possibly French'. However, in the second interview, as her future course changed and became more specific, she answered that she would use 'Japanese primarily'. She also explained her goal for learning French as follows:

> S: Initially I was hoping that, the initial plan was studying French the whole way through university ... But it's getting harder and harder, and confidence was going lower and lower. So, I just decided it would be best to stop studying, that I focus only on Japanese instead, because it was something that I could do. I could go on the JET Programme.
> I: No clear goal [for French] at this moment?
> S: No, for French. I would say it would really just be in the future the hobby language. Something like I just study for fun.

Here, although Emma was still motivated to learn French as a 'hobby language', her expectations of using the language in the future decreased partly due to the impact of her perceived career path using Japanese.

Diane (L1: English, L2: French, L3: Japanese), who also has studied French in high school and university, provided the similar comment. When asked about her goals for studying French in the first interview, Diane answered that her goal is 'to work as a translator'. However, in the second interview, she responded that her goal was 'travelling'. She decided not to pursue a French-related career because, according to her, she was not able to achieve the desired proficiency level which is required for her desired career as a translator. In contrast, Diane's goals for learning Japanese had been elaborated between the two interviews. In the first interview, she stated her goal of studying Japanese was to become a translator, but in the second interview she commented that:

> I'd like to work using Japanese. And I definitely want to go back over to Japan, visiting my family and friends again. And A University has a master's degree in translating we do a year in A University [in Australia] and a year in B University [in Japan].

Similar to Emma's case, Diane's Japanese-related goals are linked to study abroad, her career and her host family and are prioritized in her future goals.

Taken together, Emma's future self-image as a participant of the JET Programme appeared to be the central component in the early stages of the study. However, although the programme is carried out in Japan, the standard English teacher position does not require Japanese language ability. That is, her expectation to work in Japan did not necessarily help construct her career-related ideal Japanese self-image. Nonetheless, her clear goal of working in Japan appeared to contribute to her engagement in the language in and outside of the classroom and her efforts to establish personal relationships with many people through Japanese. Through the investment of her time and effort in the language (e.g. joining committee of Japanese club, using a mobile application for language learning), her current self-view as a user of the language seemed to develop. With the enhancement of her sense of self as a Japanese user, she sought out a new career paths and started to envision an ideal Japanese self as an English–Japanese translator working for a TV station. In addition, she set an academic goal (a double master's) and decided to invest in it, which helped increase the attainability and vividness of her Japanese-specific vision for the distant future. It seemed that she came to imagine successive ideal Japanese selves with different domains and timescales and that the vividness of her long-term vision was consolidated by the construction of a more feasible vision in the near future. Also, both Emma's ideal Japanese self and current Japanese self continued to develop over time, and a distance between them continued to exist. This means that her ideal Japanese self was able to maintain its motivational power.

Considering Emma's case through a DST lens, it can be said that her *ideal Japanese self-system* developed over time through dynamic interaction with other systems, such as her current Japanese self. That is, her self-image as a participant of the JET Programme appeared to be an initial attractor of her ideal Japanese self-system. Through investing in the L2, her *current Japanese self-system* was developed. The development of her current Japanese self-system contributed to a shift in her ideal Japanese self-system into a new state space where her self-image as a Japanese–English translator is a strong attractor. Further, setting new goal of taking a double master's course implies the emergence of her new ideal self-image, in which she studies translating and interpreting in Japan. With the increase in range and vividness of Emma's ideal self, her ideal Japanese self-system increased the width and depth of its *attractor basin*. Importantly, the strengthening of the subsystem (that is, the ideal Japanese self-system) also helps strengthen the larger *Japanese motivational system*.

Emma's Japanese and French motivational systems can be viewed as being in a coadapting relationship, as changes in one system bring about changes in another adjacent system. As her study of Japanese progressed, she came to have an expectation of being able to take advantage of being a native speaker of English in Japan. Partly due to the expectation, Emma shifted her investment away from French to Japanese. In other words, the coadaptation between the systems seemed to be partly influenced by a system parameter: *demands for bilingual native speakers of English* in Japan.

Laura's case

Laura (L1: English, L2: Japanese, L3: Korean, L4: Mandarin) was also brought up in an English-speaking family in Australia. In secondary school she studied Japanese for four years and enjoyed the classroom study thanks to a Japanese language teacher who consistently supported her study and underlined the importance of second language learning. As described in Chapter 4, the female teacher played a role in defining Laura's ideal self. While in secondary school, Laura visited Japan four times, including for a school trip (two weeks) and short-term (two months) and long-term (one year) exchanges. Especially in her one-year exchange, Laura enjoyed her home stay with two Japanese families, although she was initially able to speak little Japanese and the family members did not speak any English. After coming back to Australia, she maintained a close relationship with the host families. This experience appeared to have had a crucial influence not only on her persistence in learning Japanese but also on constructing her sense of self as a Japanese user (see Chapter 4). In the first interview, Laura expressed her feeling after coming back to Australia as follows:

> あの、自分の国（オーストラリアに）に戻っている時は、まだ（日本に）行っているような気持ち（でした）。… その別の国（日本）に置いてある家から出ている（ような気持ち）。家が二つあるようになって、母国も二つあるような気持ちで。

> [Well, when I came back to Australia, I felt like I was still in Japan. I felt like I went out from a home I had left in Japan. A feeling like I have two homes and two native countries.]

Laura's description of 'a feeling like I have two homes' indicates her established sense of self as a member of her Japanese host families. Indeed, she also repeated 'I want to go back to Japan' several times in the first interview (Chapter 4).

At the time of the first interview, Laura started to have a dream of becoming an interpreter, though it was not very clear. She also commented that her current goal for learning the language was to gain fluency in the use of *keigo* (Japanese honorifics). In the interview, she explained as follows:

> 今はビジネス系の日本語が話せるようになりたくて、敬語をちゃんと使える（ようになりたい）し。ビジネスとか仕事における。

[I would like to become able to speak business Japanese and properly use honorifics for business or during employment.]

During the seven months between interviews, Laura volunteered as an interpreter for a Japanese *anime* expo and also took a business Japanese class in which she was required to carry out an interview with Japanese people living in Australia using *keigo*. Through these experiences, she became more confident in speaking Japanese, and her actual self-concept as a user of the language seemed to improve. In the second interview, when asked about languages she might use for her future relationship with friends, she replied that:

それは日本語を使い続けたいなと思います。日本人の友達もいるし、ここまで（日本語学習を）応援してくれた人もいるし、私のアイデンティティの一部でもあるので。

[I think I want to continue using Japanese. This is because I have Japanese friends and there are people who have supported my study of the language until now, and also because the language is already a part of my identity.]

The above statement shows that Laura's established current self-concept (in her word, 'identity') as a Japanese user formed a solid basis for her continuing motivation for learning the language.

In addition, similar to Emma, Laura also set subsidiary goals of participating in the JET Programme and starting a master's in translation and interpretation. As mentioned, she took a business Japanese course between the interviews, and this also appeared to be influential on her projected future use of the language as the following quote exemplifies:

今授業では、日本の社内風景とか採用についても勉強しましたので。…それで（日本語学習の）ゴールが具体的に変わって。日本に働きたいならJLPTだけじゃなくて、ビジネスの日本語のいろんな能力試験がありますので、それも必要であるとわかったし。そういう具体的なゴールが出てきました。

[I have studied about the working environment and the employment in Japan… So, my goals for learning Japanese changed. I realized that if you want to work in Japan, you need to take not only JLPT but also other business-related Japanese proficiency tests. I came to have specific goals like those.]

Through seeking out a number of subordinate goals, Laura's ultimate goal of becoming a translator/interpreter appeared to become more vivid and intense. Indeed, while in the first interview, she stated that

'通訳できたらな、という夢を持っています (I have a dream of being able to interpret)', but in the second round, she expressed that 'どうしても、どうしても日本語の通訳・翻訳したいなと思ってます (I really, really want to do Japanese interpreting and translating)'. Therefore, I suggest that her current self-concept, or identity, as a Japanese user improved, and that this, as well as establishment of subsidiary goals, might help enhance the attainability of her ultimate goal of becoming a translator/interpreter and realize her wish to go back to Japan.

At university, Laura also started to learn Korean and Mandarin in addition to Japanese. In the first interview, importantly, she explained that her Japanese studies had given her a realization that she enjoys language learning and has a capability for it, which stimulated a desire to start learning Korean (see Chapter 4). Additionally, as seen in her comment that '韓国語は日本語と似ているし (because Korean is similar to Japanese)', the perceived linguistic closeness between the two languages further triggered her decision. This linguistic closeness was also a trigger for Laura's study of Mandarin, but she gradually came to realize that the distance between the two languages was larger than she initially expected.

In the first interview, Laura expressed that she was able to envisage herself as a translator using these three languages, but this vision was relatively vague. After the interview, Laura came to have more chances to communicate with Chinese people at her work place in Mandarin, and her perceived language competence in the language improved. She also continued to take Korean at the university. As a result, her Japanese, Mandarin and Korean came to increase the shared domains where these languages will be used in the future. In the first interview, when asked about languages she might use for her future leisure activities, she answered that she would use Japanese because she was fond of doing *kyūdō* (Japanese archery) and *sadō* (tea ceremony). However, in the second round, she replied to the same question differently:

その弓道・茶道をするためにやっぱり日本語が必要ですけれども、いつか教えるチャンスがあったら、オーストラリア人だけじゃなく、(中国人や韓国人にも) 中国語と韓国語を使って教える。留学生とかには教えるようになったらなと思っています。

[In order to do *kyūdō* and *sadō*, you need to use Japanese. But, if there is a chance, I can teach these things to not only Australians [but also Chinese and Korean people] in Mandarin and Korean. I think it would be great if I was able to teach international students.]

The interview extract above shows that Laura came to anticipate using the three languages not only for the career domain but also for the leisure domain of her future life.

Overall, Laura's motivational trajectory can be viewed as an upward development, similar to Emma's case. Initially, Laura's ideal self-image as a Japanese user/learner was supported by her school teacher. Her positive study abroad experiences in Japan when in high school allowed her to have an L2 identity as a member of Japanese family. The enhancement of her current L2 self-concept seemed to increase her expectation to work in Japan as a translator/interpreter, though this is not entirely certain. In university, her self-confidence in using the honorifics enhanced as she invested her time and energy in learning Japanese. Through the enhancement of her current Japanese self-concept as well as the establishment of new goals (a double master's, JET Programme and academic credentials), her career-related ideal Japanese self appeared to become more vivid and feasible. In short, her positive study experiences in high school, Japan and university helped enhance her current L2 self, which seemed to create a sound basis for the evolution of her ideal Japanese self. Importantly, there continued to exist a gap between her current and ideal L2 selves, which allowed her ideal L2 self to be an effective motivator over time. Interpreting Laura's case from a DST perspective, her *ideal Japanese self-system* was gradually developed through coadaptation with other coexisting dynamic systems, such as *Japanese learning experience* and her *current Japanese self-system*. The strengthened ideal Japanese self-system contributed to deepen the attractor basin of the larger *Japanese motivational system*.

In the first Australian study, some learners envisaged themselves using multiple languages in particular situations in the future. The data from the second interview further identified the process in which these multilingual visions, or *ideal multilingual selves* (Ushioda 2017; Henry 2017), were constructed. Somewhat similar to Emma's case, Laura's enhanced current self-concept as an L2 (Japanese) user contributed to the emergence of L3 (Korean) and L4 (Mandarin) motivational systems. However, unlike Emma, Laura came to anticipate that the future use of L3 and L4 were subsidiary but complimentary to her L2-related ideal career. As she invested in learning the three languages, she came to envision herself using all the languages for not only future employment but also future leisure activities. That is, she started constructing an ideal multilingual self that is linked to a number of life domains.

DST conceives of that newly developed dynamic systems tend to show a higher variability than older systems, which are generally more stable (Verspoor 2015).

On the one hand, Emma's ideal French and Japanese self-systems were relatively newly developed and did not appear to share a common component. On the other hand, Laura's newly developed ideal Mandarin and Korean self-systems appeared to gravitate to the *attractor state* of the older and more stable ideal Japanese self-system, sharing common attractors like an ideal self that is related to career and leisure domains. As a result of the coadaptation between Laura's Japanese, Korean and Mandarin motivational systems, the new, higher level *ideal multilingual self-system* seemed to emerge. It appears that the combination of Laura's L2, L3 and L4, which can all be classified as Asian languages, helped her construct an ideal multilingual self (or self as an Asian expert) more easily. In contrast, the combination of Emma's European (French) and Asian (Japanese) languages did not greatly help the construction of her multilingual vision with the distance between these languages appearing to hamper the construction. Therefore, the coadapting process between Laura's ideal L2, L3 and L4 self-systems and the emergence of a new dynamic multilingual self-system might be, in part, facilitated by the overlapping linguistic and cultural aspects of her chosen languages.

Waning motivational trajectory

Compared with sustained motivational trajectory, *waning motivational trajectory* can be characterized as a motivational decline due to the achievement, or diminishment, of the ideal L2 self. In this section, Iseok and Scott's cases will be presented because of their distinct cultural and linguistic backgrounds and differing motives to study Japanese. Whereas Iseok's interest in Japanese pop culture had been the important driving force behind his study of the language, Scott's initial study of the L2 was primary motivated by his strong desire to travel to Japan.

Iseok's case

At the time of the first interview, Iseok (L1: Korean, L2: English, L3: Japanese, L4: Mandarin) was a third-year student in his first semester and had two years left before graduation. Similar to the Korean participants, he was born in South Korea and studied English as a compulsory subject at primary and secondary schools for five years. His motive to study English was derived from a general belief in Korean society about the importance of English in future success (cf. Park 2009), and his future goal for learning the language was unclear (Chapter 4). Iseok came to Australia when he was fifteen years of age. Initially, because of his limited knowledge and skills in English, living in the country was quite challenging. The following statement indicates his concerted effort to acquire the language:

> （オーストラリアに着いた）その後は、ここの生活のために、生き残るために英語が必要なんだと思って。... 必死に英語を勉強するようになりました。
>
> [After arriving at Australia, I began to study English very hard ... because I realized that English is necessary to live and survive here.]

Iseok decided to major in law and science in university and started to think of his future career as a lawyer who uses English. It seemed that English became a dominant language in the education and career domains of his future life. In the first interview, he expressed his intention to continue with learning English by stating that '英語を使う仕事をやっている限り、死ぬまで続けると思います (I think that as long as I'm involved in an English-related career I will continue to learn English until I die)'.

Before coming to Australia, Iseok was interested in Japanese and learned the language as a 'hobby' through translating Japanese pop songs into Korean language and posting them on the Internet. As he pursued the hobby for two years, his proficiency in the language dramatically enhanced, and he passed the second highest level of the JLPT (N2). However, he did not consider future use of the language:

> I: その当時、高校の時に日本語を将来使うと思っていましたか？
> S: いつか自分の力になるとは思いましたけど、専攻になるとは保証できなかったんです。…高校の時、将来何をするか、あんまり興味をもってませんでした。
>
> [I: At that time, did you think you will use Japanese in the future?
> S: I did think that it will be useful one day, but I wasn't sure whether I would major in it ... When in high school, I didn't care about what I should do in the future.]

Since Iseok was not successful in science in the first year of university, he decided to take Japanese as an alternative major. As seen in Chapter 4, he chose Japanese partly because of his perceived ease and self-confidence in the language. He gradually came to believe that it might be advantageous for him to be able to use Japanese in addition to English for his career path as a patent lawyer. However, this future goal was vague, meaning that his career-related ideal Japanese self had a limited motivational power.

In the second interview, Iseok stated that his motivation for learning Japanese had dropped over time. It seemed that his perceived decline in the motivation was largely due to the fact that he had already attained his desired proficiency level in Japanese and was satisfied with it and because of his unclear future goal. The following interview extracts represent this trend:

> 昔は本とか読むために、そうじゃないと音楽を聞くために（日本語を）勉強しましたが、今はまあ全然問題ありませんので。… 今は（日本語学習のゴールは）特にありません。
>
> [In the past, I studied Japanese in order to read books or to listen to the music, but now I can do this with no problems … So, I now don't have any particular goal for learning the language.]
>
> （モチベーションは）そんなに高くありません。… まあ生活の一部になっているから、勉強としてやらなくてもいいかなと思って。接するだけで十分かなと思ってます、今は。だからモチベーションとして高くありませんね。
>
> [My motivation for learning Japanese is not very high … I think I don't need to 'study' the language because it is a part of my life. At this moment, I think it is enough for me to be expose to the language. So, as for my motivation, it is not high.]

As Iseok's utterance 'it is a part of my life' indicates, the achievement of his goal of being able to enjoy Japanese pop culture helped establish his current self-concept as a Japanese user. After the achievement, however, his future L2 goal/ideal L2 self, did not seem to be revised. In the second interview, he reported that he currently had around twenty people to communicate with in Japanese on a regular basis. That is, despite his lack of motivation for learning, Japanese was still clearly an important part of his life. He expressed his intention to continue with using the language as follows:

> 日本語もたぶんずっと続けると思います。今も周りの人とか知り合いがぜんぜん日本語を使うようになっているから。… その関係が続く限りは。それに私がこの趣味（pop culture）を続ける限りは、ずっと続けると思います。
>
> [I will probably continue with Japanese for a long time. Because currently people around me and my friends came to use Japanese … As long as I keep the

relationship with them, or as long as I continue this hobby [pop culture], I think I will continue with using Japanese.]

Thus, while Iseok's interest in pop culture and his firmly established current self-concept as a user of Japanese allowed him to anticipate *using* the language in the future, his current motivation for *learning* the language appeared to decrease, partly due to the lack of motivational power of his ideal L2 self.

Altogether, the initial driving force of Iseok's study of Japanese was his interest in Japanese pop culture. On the basis of his interest, his ideal Japanese self (a future self-image in which he enjoys Japanese songs without translations) was constructed. Iseok's ideal Japanese self, which is linked to the leisure domain, was achieved and integrated into his current self with the enhancement of his current self-view as a Japanese user. Afterwards, however, Iseok seemed to stop envisioning further extension of his ideal self-image, and his ideal and current L2 self-images came to have little distance between them. From a DST perspective, Iseok's *interest in Japanese culture* was an important attractor of his *Japanese motivational system*, which can also be characterized as an initial condition of the system. The initial condition helped the development of his *ideal Japanese self-system*. However, with the achievement of his ideal self-image, Iseok's ideal Japanese self-system appeared to be thrown out of an *attractor state* and into a *repeller state*. With the wane of the subsystem (ideal Japanese self-system), Iseok's Japanese motivational system seemed to weaken despite that another important subsystem (interest in L2) was sustained. Here, it is important to note that while the achievement of Iseok's ideal Japanese self-image brought about the weakening of his Japanese motivational system, it also helped strengthen his *current Japanese self-system*. This is reflected in his established self-concept as a Japanese user and strong intention to continue to use Japanese for a long time.

In contrast to Iseok's Japanese motivational system, the initial conditions of his *English motivational system* might be represented by his sense of obligation to learn the language, which is associated with his ought-to English self in the career domain. Also, the system's movement appeared to be governed by a system parameter, namely, *demands for English as a career language* (see Chapter 5). After arriving in Australia, an English-speaking country, as his earlier utterance about 'survival' indicates, his English motivational system shifted into a new attractor state where demands for English exercise a decisive impact on the system. As he decided to major in law at university and started to dream of becoming a lawyer, a new attractor, his ideal English self linked to education and career domains, emerged. In other words, according to changes of environment and life phases, the attractor basin of his English motivational system dramatically increased in width and depth. This caused the system to stabilize in a new state space. It seems that the development of Iseok's *ideal English self-system*, where his career-related self-image is a strong attractor, partly restrict the development of his ideal Japanese self-system.

Scott's case

When Scott (L1: English, L2: Japanese, L3: Indonesian) was interviewed for the first time, he was a third-year student in his second semester and had around a year and a half left before graduation. When he started to learn Japanese in secondary school, he enjoyed the study largely because of his wish to communicate with his 'favourite teachers', all of whom were Japanese and supported his study (see Chapter 4). During this time, he visited Japan twice. Although he did not often imagine himself using Japanese for his future employment, he had a strong wish to travel and live in Japan, as he explained in the first interview:

> S: Well, I guess I was used to the Australian environment. I wanted something different, and I think there's different opportunities, and like lots of fun ... at Japan.
> I: So, for travelling?
> S: Yeah, for travelling and meeting people.

Scott decided to continue with the language in university because of his desires to be fluent enough to communicate with people and to not waste the time and energy invested in the language (Chapter 4). In the university, however, he experienced difficulties in learning the language and consequently failed one Japanese course. According to him, this was due to the gap between his personal preference for speaking/communication and the institutional focus on writing/grammar, explaining that 'unfortunately for me, the style of teaching in university isn't best suited to me'.

Before the first interview, Scott visited Japan for one month (with his friends for two weeks and with his family for two weeks). As shown in his statement regarding this trip, this boosted his motivation for learning Japanese:

> Yeah, it was good 'cause no one could really speak much Japanese. I do everything, yeah ... A few nights, I even went out just by myself, not with my family, and I found little *izakaya* [bar] ... And if there was no *gaijin* [foreigner], and then

I go in. So, speak Japanese all night, and drink some *shōchū*. Good! Just tried to practice. And it would be fun if I could always have conversations. Good fun.

Scott's experience in Japan not only increased his desire to travel and communicate with Japanese people but also seemed to help him project future usage of Japanese. The following two statements from the first interview exemplify this trend:

> I think I want to try to find a job, maybe ski fields for like a few months, and then in the city... tutoring English or something for a few months.

> And I really want to work at the Olympics somehow, because, Tokyo 2020 ... Obviously they need bilingual speakers for Japanese and English. So, I could get job there somehow. *Suikyū* (water polo) team. Just like a translator or interpreter or just helping out with everything, yeah.

Also, Scott's travel experience in Japan appeared to contribute to maintaining his self-confidence in Japanese and motivation for studying the language at university:

> So, I, the end of every semester studying Japanese at uni, I go 'Oh, suck Japanese', because I don't do well. And then I lose a bit my motivation ... But then, because I spent a month there [in Japan], my friends like ... 'Oh, how do you speak Japanese? *Jōzu desune. Perapera desune* [Your Japanese is so good! You're so fluent!]'. So, [that] let me have really high confidence what I got back.

Ultimately, while Scott lost his self-confidence in academic Japanese through low results at the university, he appeared to maintain his confidence in communicative Japanese. Indeed, in both interviews he stated that he is 'very confident' in the language.

As Japanese was his minor subject, Scott stopped studying the language at university after the first interview. In the second interview, he commented that he still envisaged himself using Japanese for casual works in Japan such as an interpreter for the Tokyo 2020 Olympics and working as an English teacher. However, there seemed to be little evidence that his ideal Japanese self-image had changed or been elaborated since the first interview. Despite his self-perceived high confidence in conversational Japanese, he clearly stated that his current motivation for studying the language had dropped.

It was just before the first interview that Scott started to study Indonesian at his university. Although he was a beginner learner of the language, he believed that it is easier for him to get to higher levels of proficiency in Indonesian compared with Japanese:

I'm very confident [in Indonesian], I think. Especially, one of the things I found challenging in Japanese was the *kanji*, and also the alphabet, but Indonesian is just the same letters [as English]. And because of that I can learn it orally and orally, just by speaking. So, I think I probably have more potential to learn Indonesian quickly.

Scott had a close friend to communicate with once every two weeks who lives in Indonesia. He described the friend as the most significant person in his study of the language. Through communicating with her, he decided to do an internship in Indonesia for a few months. He also planned to go on an exchange to Malaysia where people speak Malay, which is very close to Indonesian. In the next semester, he stopped taking Japanese courses and had more opportunities to study and use Indonesian. As a result of his investment in Indonesian, he started to perceive the future utility of the language in the interpersonal and career domains of his life. In the second interview, he said, 'I'm hoping to go to the internship in January and maybe do a little more work over there [Indonesia] for a little bit'.

In the second interview, Scott also commented that his perceived confidence and competence in Indonesian, as well as motivation for learning the language, increased in the seven-month period:

I was interested in March and I've just started doing it. So, I was quite motivated. But, motivation has changed because I need to be good at it. Clear goal and purpose of actually going over.

In seeking future employment, Scott appeared to perceive an advantage of being a native speaker of English, which is similar to Emma's case. However, unlike Emma, who believed there were stronger possibilities of getting a job in Japan than in France, Scott considered it relatively easy to seek employment in both Japan and Indonesia. He explained his plan after graduation as follows:

It's probably, it's very similar for both Indonesian and Japanese. I hope to travel a lot and live in both areas and try to improve my language a lot. Because I love the idea of living and working overseas, like a big holiday ... But, in the nearest future, I think just travelling and working, maybe teaching English in those countries [Japan and Indonesia], because there is a potential because I can speak English.

It seems to be easy for Scott to anticipate a future where he uses Japanese or Indonesian at work. However, his possible future paths are not permanent but always related to casual employment like a part-time job (e.g. ski resort, interpreter in the Tokyo 2020 Olympics, English teacher). Furthermore, as his utterance 'like a big holiday' indicates, this possible future work in Japan or Indonesia was closely related to his strong wish to travel to these countries.

Overall, Scott's relationship with his high school teachers and his positive travel experience in Japan seemed to help boost his interest in Japanese culture. These experiences also helped him possess a great self-confidence in travelling and communicating with people in Japanese. Scott came to project future usage of the language for short-term employment in Japan. However, since the expected future employment, which can be viewed as an extension of the travel, did not require higher proficiency in Japanese, there seemed to be little distance between his current and ideal Japanese self-images. Furthermore, because of the difficulties he faced in his study of Japanese, Scott's ideal L2 self, which is linked to education and career domains, seemed to be perceived as unattainable and therefore vague. Scott's future Japanese self was not revised upwardly and had a limited motivational power. It seemed that the wane in his motivation for learning Japanese was partly due to the lack of motivating capacity from his ideal L2 self. In their study, which investigated Australian university students' reasons to continue/discontinue Japanese study, Northwood and Thomson (2012) found that the difficulty of Japanese in relation to the writing system is the second highest reason for the students' discontinuation. The present study supports this finding and further suggests that the difficulty of Japanese may also contribute to reduce the vividness and attainability of the students' ideal L2 self.

In DST terms, Scott's Japanese motivational system was initially lodged in an *attractor state*, where his *interest in L2 culture* was a strong attractor which considerably influenced subsequent behaviour of the system. Scott's current Japanese self-system, which was developed through his positive L2 use experiences in Japan, appeared to facilitate the development of his *ideal Japanese self-system*. However, partly due to the difficulties of learning the L2, his ideal Japanese self became vague. This means that his ideal Japanese self-system weakened, having a narrow and shallow basin of attractor. Similar to Iseok's case, with the weakening of the subsystem (ideal Japanese self), Scott's *Japanese motivational system* also weakened.

During the period between the two interviews, Scott started to invest his time and energy not only in Japanese but also in Indonesian. He seemed to consider that his linguistic capital (L1 English) helps make possible his ambition of travelling in Japan or Indonesia and continuing to learn the languages. However, unlike Laura, who invested in L3 Korean and L4 Mandarin on the basis of her L2 Japanese, and thereby constructed an ideal multilingual self, Scott's investment in L3 Indonesian seemed to have little to do with his L2 Japanese. His ideal L2 and L3 self-images did not appear to be in a cooperating relationship. From a DST perspective, it seemed that his ideal Japanese and Indonesian self-systems developed by the influence of a system parameter: *demands for bilingual native speakers of English*. However, both systems made little coadaptation. As was discussed in Laura's case, this may be partly because Scott's old ideal L2 (Japanese) self-system was not developed sufficiently to attract his new ideal L3 (Indonesian) self-system. Alternatively, the combination of Japanese and Indonesian did not greatly facilitate the construction of his ideal multilingual self-image due to the little linguistic/cultural overlap between these languages.

Chapter summary

This chapter sought to examine the dynamic development of the Australian participants' motivation(s) for learning Japanese. Through the analysis, two motivational trajectories that were not identical to those of the Korean study were detected, along with underlying mechanisms in the trajectories. First, one of the initial conditions of the participants' Japanese motivational system(s) was characterized as an *interest in Japanese language/culture*, which is derived from the perceived linguistic/cultural distance between Japanese and their first language and/or their positive L2 use/learning experiences. Here, their interest in Japanese culture can be roughly divided into (1) interest in pop culture, and (2) interest in travelling/communicating with people. This tendency was somewhat different from the Korean context, where interest in travelling/communicating with people was not identified as the initial condition of any informant's Japanese motivational system. Secondly, while many Korean participants' Japanese motivational systems appeared to weaken over time, those of the Australian participants showed a more consistent tendency toward strengthening. Here, whether they had successful Japanese learning experience or not had a great influence on the development of their ideal Japanese selves and motivation to learn the language, which is consistent with the findings from the Korean study. Thirdly, the system parameter of *demands for bilingual native speakers of English* in Japan was found to guide the behaviour of many participants' Japanese motivational systems, as well as how these systems interacted with other L2 motivational systems. This parameter stands in clear contrast to the one identified in the Korean context (*demands for English as a career language*). The importance and implications of these findings will be further discussed in the following chapter.

7

Language learning motivation in English-speaking and non-English-speaking contexts

This chapter compares and contrasts the main findings from both the Korean studies (Chapters 3 and 5) and Australian studies (Chapters 4 and 6) and draws some conclusions. First, it reports a number of important aspects of Japanese language learners' L2 self and other related motivational factors. In particular, it discusses the concept of domain of possible selves as a useful framework to analyze motivation for learning LOTEs, which potentially have more varied aspects than does English, as well as the complex relationship between different language-specific visions within the learner. It also considers the significant impact of feared L2 self of L1 English speakers on their motivation to learn LOTEs, which has previously not received much attention. The second part of the chapter discusses differing impacts of Global English (as an L2 and as an L1) on motivation to learn additional languages and on the construction of an ideal self as a multilingual user. The third section of the chapter examines the signature dynamics of both sustained and waning motivational trajectories. Finally, on the basis of the above results, the chapter provides pedagogical implications, suggestions for future research and brief concluding remarks.

Motivation to learn LOTE

Domain of L2 self

Based on the findings from the Korean and Australian studies, I argue that possible future L2 self is developed within projected future use in particular life domains. As Emma and Laura's cases showed, L2 learners envision ideal L2 self in different time scales and distinct life domains, and the domains often shift as their study progresses. Initially, many participants had a strong interest in

Japanese language/culture but did not seem to possess a clear vision of an ideal Japanese self. Through various Japanese learning/use experiences in high school and in Japan (e.g. travel, study abroad), their ideal Japanese selves connected to particular life domains appeared to emerge. In both Korean and Australian contexts, leisure domain (e.g. enjoying pop culture) was important at school, and career domain became more of focus as they progressed in their degrees. This is correspondent to Markus and Nurius's (1986) argument that the nature of individuals' future self-guides varies depending on their position in the life span. In the field of L2 motivation, Csizér and Kormos (2009) also claim that the motivational impact of ideal L2 self changes depending on life stages. Especially for university language learners, whether or not they can envisage a career-related ideal L2 self may be a crucial element which influences the development of their motivation for learning the language.

Bi/multilingual studies have claimed that 'bilinguals usually acquire and use their languages for different purposes, in different domains of life, with different people' (Grosjean 2008: 23). Possible selves research (e.g. Unemori, Omoregie and Markus 2004) in psychology also has focused on the discrepancy between current and future self-representations linked to a particular domain (e.g. academic, career, health). Language learning motivation research, however, have not placed much importance on the classification of life domain to which one's L2 self is linked. This may be partly because in second language acquisition (SLA) research learner's L2 self-concept has been often categorized as one of the academic self-concepts (see Mercer 2011; Mills 2014: 10). Alternatively, it may be because L2 motivation research has mainly focused on the study of English, which is very likely to be connected to career domain (cf. Kim 2009; Irie and Brewster 2015). Needless to say, *domain of L2 self* is just an analytical concept, and in reality, the border between the domains may be vague and fluid, as our life domains are often overlapped or mixed. Yet, especially when investigating LOTE learners' L2 self, it is beneficial to focus not only on the ideal/ought-to dimension but also on the domain that the L2 self in question is linked to. This is because, as the present study reported, motivation for learning LOTEs potentially have more varied aspects than that for English. Dörnyei and Al-Hoorie's (2017: 465) also point out that, compared with English, LOTEs are more likely to be associated with very specific and personalized reasons, as well as a specific community where the L2 is spoken. In addition, the concept of domain of L2 self is highly useful when investigating the coadaptation between different language-specific visions and thus the development of ideal multilingual self within a learner.

The second Korean and Australian studies further indicated that the concept of domain of L2 self is well suited to the analysis based on Dynamic Systems Theory (DST). In respect to the relationship between L2 and L3 self-images within a learner, some cases (e.g. Anbok, Scott) showed that L2 and L3 self-representations were connected to different domains of future life, whereas other cases (e.g. Oyeon, Laura) indicated that L2 and L3 selves were linked to the same domain, constructing a multilingual vision. Considering these characteristics in terms of DST, the range of domain of ideal L2 self is related to the width of attractor basin of ideal L2 self-system. That is, when a learner envisions her/his ideal L2 self which is linked to a wider range of domains, her/his ideal L2 self-system has a more varied range of initial conditions, or a wider basin of attraction, meaning that the system can easily be propelled by events into the attractor state (Hiver 2015: 24). Also, when a learner imagines a multilingual vision linked to a particular domain, her/his ideal L2 and L3 self-systems share a deeper attractor basin and thus have a greater stability.

Achievement of ideal L2 self

The present study also found that when an ideal L2 self is achieved, it is validated and incorporated into current L2 self and thus loses its motivational power. An Australian informant (with a Korean background), Iseok, displayed a waning motivational trajectory despite having been a highly motivated and successful student in the past. He appeared to lose motivation for learning Japanese after having achieved his ideal self, in which he enjoys Japanese pop songs without translation. While the achievement brought about the enhancement of his current Japanese self-concept, his ideal Japanese self was not updated or reproduced. A Korean informant, Anbok, who is categorized in sustaining motivational trajectory, also perceived a decrease in motivation for learning Japanese after attaining the highest certificate of JLPT. In his case, however, after the attainment he continued to look for an alternative goal. Anbok's ideal Japanese self was validated and incorporated into the repertoire of current selves, and after that it was still updated (cf. Dunkel, Kelts and Coon 2006: 189).

From a DST point of view, the difference between the two cases is partly related to the initial conditions of their Japanese motivational systems. On the one hand, the fact that Iseok did not choose to major in Japanese when entering university indicates that his ideal Japanese self-system was mainly connected to the leisure domain and thus had a narrow attractor basin. With the attainment of his goal of enjoying Japanese pop culture without subtitles, the system shifted from an attractor state to a repeller state. On the other hand, Anbok's ideal Japanese self, which is linked to a very specific goal (N1) in the education domain, was an initial strong attractor of his Japanese motivational system. With the achievement of the certificate, the system was thrown to a repeller state. However, since the initial attractor was so strong, and he was also in a situation (enrolled in a major) which demanded that he continues his study, the system sought out a new attractor state which is also governed by a powerful attractor (i.e. ideal Japanese self which is linked to travel).

Previous studies (e.g. You, Dörnyei and Csizér 2015; Henry 2012; Mercer 2011) have revealed some dynamic aspects of L2 self, such as: (1) up- and downward revisions, (2) changes triggered by other L2 self-concepts and (3) qualitative/quantitative changes in the imagery. Yet, the development of L2 self after being achieved, or not being achieved, has not been fully explored (cf. Irie and Ryan 2015: 358). The current study contributed to the understanding of how individual L2 learners sustain motivation and how they approach L2 learning after the achievement of an initial goal (or ideal L2 self) through the perspective of DST. As Iseok's case indicates, L2 learners who have already achieved their ideal L2 selves may lose an important motivational source. However, their current L2 self-concepts which are constructed through the achievement of their ideal L2 selves may help them keep using the language.

Feared L2 self

Because of the perceived difficulty and required investment of time and effort to learn Japanese, five Australian participants reported that they have a fear of losing their language skills, which was a driving force in the language learning (Chapter 4). They appeared to believe that they should not waste their valuable L2 competence and imagine their feared selves, in which they lose ability in the L2. It is believed that one's ideal L2 self can be most effective when it is offset by one's feared self in the same domain (Dörnyei 2009). Thus, the construction of the Australian informants' ideal Japanese selves may be partly reinforced by their feared Japanese selves. While L1 English speakers have an increasing difficulty in learning additional languages and a motivational disadvantage in the era of Global English (Lanvers 2016), due to the significant investment the Australian informants have already made, they are more likely to envisage their feared L2 selves in addition to ideal L2 selves, which enables them to have a greater energizing potential.

Feared self, in definition, is similar to ought-to self as both are on 'prevention-focus' (Markus and Nurius 1986), but the two concepts are qualitatively different from each other. Ought-to self is constructed through pressure from other people (Higgins 1987), whereas feared self is more grounded in personal experience (Hoyle and Sherrill 2006). Given that the Australian informants provided more evidence of their feared Japanese selves than their ought-to Japanese selves, I argue that for the better understanding of L1 English speakers' language learning motivation, their feared L2 selves should be more focused upon.

L2 learning experience

The data showed that the Korean and Australian informants' different L2 learning experiences have different impacts on their motivational trajectories. First of all, for those four Australian informants (Laura, Debra, Diane and Susan), who studied in Japan when in high school, their study abroad experiences not only brought about long-lasting relationships with their host families/friends but also enhanced their current identity as a member of a Japanese family or community. Even for the other two participants (Emma, Scott) who did not have a study abroad experience, their pleasant experiences of travel in Japan helped them broaden their horizons and have an expectation to use Japanese in the future (Chapter 4). Kurata (2004) argues that L2 learners' in-country experience has continuing positive effects on their L2 learning even after coming back to their home country. That is, after their sojourn experiences, learners tend to establish more developed relationships with native speakers of the L2, and use the L2 more frequently. Therefore, the Australian participants' active participation in various Japan-related activities and their generally vivid ideal Japanese self-images may be partly rooted to their positive learning experiences of the language in Japan. In addition, since their positive in-country experiences were mainly reported by the participants in the group of *monolingual* English speakers, it is possible that a larger linguistic/cultural distance between English and Japanese provides the learners with a great possibility to broaden their understanding and perspective through their stay in Japan. Additionally, this trend may reflect Japanese people's more favourable attitudes toward Western-background foreigners than Asian-background foreigners. Siegal (1996) pointed out that Westerners who speak Japanese proficiently tend to be admired by some native speakers. In this sense, the Australian participants in *monolingual* group are more likely to have pleasant experiences while sojourning in Japan than those in the other groups as well as their Korean counterparts.

Not only in-country experience, but L2 learning experience in university was also shown to have a strong impact on the development of current and ideal Japanese self-images. Laura and Emma's cases showed that positive L2 learning experiences, such as participation in Japanese club and business Japanese course, help enhance one's current self-image as an L2 user (Chapter 6). As the distance between current and ideal L2 selves has diminished and the ideal L2 self becomes more likely, these informants appeared to upgrade their ideal L2 self in the light of new study and career options, which facilitates further experience of L2 learning. In contrast, Minseop and Cheonga's cases demonstrated that a lack of Japanese use/learning experience had a negative impact on their expectation to use the language in the future. Within the framework of the L2 Motivational Self System, the concept of L2 learning experience has been viewed as primary related to the institutional impact on L2 motivation (e.g. the teacher, the curriculum, the peer group, the experience of success), whereas the impact of L2 *use* experience outside of the classroom has been paid little attention. Examining L2-related experience both in- and outside of the classroom might be necessary to uncover the whole picture of motivation for learning LOTEs, which are often associated with a specific community outside of institution (Dörnyei and Al-Hoorie 2017).

Interest in L2 language/culture

In both Korean and Australian contexts, the informants' *interest in L2 language/culture* was one of the most significant elements in their motivation for learning Japanese. As far as the informants of the present study are concerned, their intrinsic interest in Japanese culture can be roughly divided into either interest in the pop culture or interest in travelling/communicating with people. For some informants, whose interest in Japanese culture is related to the pop culture, their intrinsic interest enables them to have various L2 experiences (e.g. listening to Japanese pop songs, watching TV dramas and joining online forums) which help develop their current identity as a Japanese user in the leisure domain. For the other informants, whose interest in the L2 culture is rooted to their travel or study experience in Japan, their interest may help them have further Japanese-related experiences (e.g. travelling, communicating with Japanese people) which contributes to enhance their current Japanese self in the leisure and interpersonal domains. Here, interest in travelling/communicating with people can be seen as what has traditionally been called *integrative motivation* (Gardner 1985), since it assumes one's willingness to participate in social interaction with members of other groups.

In DST terms, interest plays a significant role as an *initial condition* of the participants' Japanese motivational system and influences the subsequent movement of the system (Verspoor 2015). The following statement by Pilho best describes that his interest in Japanese pop culture functions as an attractor to which his Japanese motivational system gravitates:

> （日本語の）課題や授業などで、「しなければならない」からやる気は出すしかありません。それでストレスを受けて楽しさが下がるわけです。しかし、趣味として日本のドラマや漫画、本、ゲームなどに触れながら、時々「あ、翻訳とか要らないから楽だな、日本語勉強してよかった」と思うことがあります。そのとき、日本語に対する楽しさが回復できます。

> [I have to generate my motivation because I 'have to' do Japanese assignments and attend the class. Thus, my enjoyment decreases due to the stress. But, when I watch or read Japanese TV dramas, books, games and things like that for pleasure, I sometimes feel like, 'Oh, it's enjoyable for me that I don't need the translation. I'm glad that I have studied Japanese', which revives my interest in the language.]

According to Dörnyei and Ushioda (2011: 92), interest is a 'motivational conglomerate' which includes motivational, cognitive and affective factors. Waninge (2015) further argues that whereas ideal L2 self is a motivational conglomerate which can stabilize one's L2 motivational system on a longer timescale, interest is a conglomerate which acts on a shorter timescale. The present study, however, found that the participants' interest in Japanese language/culture exerted a long-term influence on their engagement and persistence in learning the L2. This argument is supported by Ryan and Deci (2003: 255) who point out that 'in some cases, identities appear to grow directly from natural inclinations, interests, and curiosities... [E]arly experiences of intrinsic motivation supply the impetus for a person's choice of an avocation, career, or lifestyle that ultimately becomes part of his or her identity'.

That is, the informants' interest in Japanese language/culture can feature not only in their current Japanese self-concept (e.g. as a J-pop listener, as a gamer) but also in their future self-representations as Japanese users, which influences their motivation for learning the language. Yet, in the later years of tertiary education in particular, one's ideal L2 self, which is derived from ones' interest in L2, may have less motivational power than that which is linked to the career domain. This may be because the former is often linked to the leisure or interpersonal domain which does not require as high levels of L2 proficiency as the latter (see

Iseok's case in Chapter 6). More importantly, it reflects the fact that personal interest is often not the major focus during tertiary study, where career goals become the primary focus.

Nonetheless, interest in Japanese language/culture does have a stable and long-term effect on the informants' motivation for learning the language. Studies in motivation for learning languages, in general, and LOTEs, in particular, need to conceive of intrinsic interest in the target language/culture as an important motivational element, or conglomerate, which acts on both shorter and longer timescales and often provides the base for other motivations to develop.

Motivation across multiple languages

Impact of Global English

The present study makes a significant contribution to our understanding of motivation across multiple languages, which is an area of growing interest in the field of SLA. In both Korean and Australian contexts, the impact of Global English was identified as an important factor which influences the participants' motivation for learning Japanese, but in different ways related to its status as L1 or L2. Some Korean informants stated that they would continue with learning English after graduation, instead of Japanese, suggesting that they would shift their investment away from Japanese to English. Even in the case of Oyeon, who seems to be the most enthusiastic Japanese learner among the participants, because of the high demand for English in the Korean job market, English came to be given a higher priority than Japanese in terms of her future employment during the seven-month period. As Park (2009: 238) argues, due to the language ideologies of English which are articulated and circulated in Korean society, 'English is perceived to be a language of globalization, a force which Korea must embrace in order to survive in the global economy'. As the participants entered university and came to focus more on their future employment, they sought to generate *linguistic capital* (Bourdieu and Passeron 1990) through learning English. The perceived great utility of English seemed to have a negative impact on setting their long-term learning goals for Japanese and on the construction, or revision, of their ideal Japanese selves.

From a DST perspective, in Korea, *demands for English as a career language* (the social recognition that English is necessary for one's successful future) can be seen as one of the system parameters of the informants' English (L2) and Japanese (L3) motivational systems, influencing the coadaptation between these systems. For some informants, it contributed to the strengthening of their English motivational system and the weakening of their Japanese motivational system, as noted previously. For the others, however, it facilitated a more constructive coadaptation between the systems and promoted the emergence of a dynamic system at a higher level, namely their multilingual (English, Japanese and Korean) vision. These findings may be applicable to other LOTEs learning contexts around the world, where target language is taught simultaneously with, or subsequently to, English.

Unlike their Korean counterparts, most of the Australian informants already have native or near-native competence in English, which is valuable linguistic capital. Lanvers (2016) says that in many Anglophone countries, such as Australia, monolingual English speakers' awareness of the importance of Global English may impede their motivation for learning L2. The author points out that on the macro level, the lower status of the L2 than L1, the low perceived capital gain and the low priority given to language learning hamper their language learning. As far as the Australian participants in the present study are concerned, however, this is not the case. The participants are able to invest their language-learning efforts in the acquisition of other languages in which they have a personal interest. Also, many of them take advantage of being native English speakers for their study of Japanese. Especially after entering university, they came to know that there is a high demand for native English speakers in Japan. As L1 English speakers, they are able to have various options after graduation, which are predicated on knowledge of English and Japanese, such as the JET Programme and a double master's. These elements might all help not only set long-term learning goals and upgrade their ideal/feared self-images as Japanese users/learners but also construct a bilingual vision, in which they speak both English and Japanese. In contrast, after entering university, two (Emma and Diane) of the informants' ideal French self-images, which were primarily connected to the leisure domain (e.g. French literature), came to have a weak link to the career domain, partly because of the relatively low demands for English speakers such as themselves in France.

Therefore, in Australia, *demands for bilingual native speakers of English* in Japan appeared to be one of the system parameters, which mediate the coadapting process between the informants' L2 and L3 motivational systems. For some informants, the parameter not only influenced the strengthening of their Japanese motivational system and promoting their bilingual visions but also contributed to the weakening of their French motivational system. These findings can also be applied to other LOTE learning contexts in English-speaking countries, such as the USA and the UK.

To sum up, depending on its status as L2 or L1, Global English, as a system parameter, has different impacts on the development of LOTE learner's motivational system. An important lesson drawn from the findings is, however, that the impact of the system parameters is neither entirely positive nor negative. Rather, the parameters facilitate continuing interaction between different L2/L3/L4 motivational systems, which can sometimes result in the emergence of a dynamic system at a higher level (bi/multilingual vision), which will be discussed in the following sections.

Construction of ideal multilingual self

All the participants have at least a bilingual vision, and some of them have a multilingual vision, consisting of three or more languages. While the concept of the *multilingual self* (Pavlenko 2006: 1) represents multilingual's current self-perception, the current study uses a term, *ideal multilingual self*, which refers to one's ideal future self-image in which one uses two or more languages within particular domains of life. The topic of multilingual vision is starting to gain attention, which is reflected in the special issue of *The Modern Language Journal* ('Beyond Global English: Motivation to Learn Languages in a Multicultural World') edited by Ushioda and Dörnyei (2017). While a few scholars (Ushioda 2017; Henry 2017) in the volume have proposed theoretical and practical implications of the concept of *ideal multilingual self*, dynamic development of this construct has not been adequately investigated. There has been a controversial question of whether a bi/multilingual speaker has different self-concepts in different languages or a single self-concept. However, as Pavlenko (2006: 6) rightly posits, a uniform answer to the question may be neither possible nor desirable. In some circumstances, bi/multilinguals may see their language selves as different, but in other situations, they may feel that they have a single or hybrid self-concept. In a similar vein, some bi/multilinguals may envision their ideal multilingual selves in which different language-specific self-concepts are perceived to be separated, but others may imagine hybrid multilingual visions. As far as the informants of the present study are concerned, several appeared to have ideal multilingual selves, in which different language-specific self-concepts are blended harmoniously.

During the period between the two interviews, Oyeon's ideal self-image as a researcher, in which she speaks mainly L3 Japanese, shifted into a more vivid ideal self-image as a translator, in which she uses L2 English, L3 Japanese, L4 Mandarin and L1 Korean in that order of priority (Chapter 5). Another informant who envisioned an ideal self-image as a multilingual user was Junha (L1: Korean, L2: English, L3: Japanese). In his case, his ultimate goal of being a diplomat, who speaks mainly English and also other languages (e.g. Japanese), was already set before entering the university. After the first interview, he set a short-term goal of taking a master's degree of international relations after graduation, which helped increase the attainability and elaborateness of his ideal multilingual self in the distant future (Chapter 3). From a DST perspective, these informants' multilingual vision, which can be viewed as a dynamic system at a higher level, emerged through the coadaptation between their L2, L3 (and L4 in Oyeon's case) motivational systems.

In Australia, five (Laura, Scott, Luyue, Yian and Iseok) out of twelve participants were learning other languages in addition to Japanese at university, and four of them chose to study Mandarin or/and Korean (Chapter 4). Laura imagined her ideal multilingual self, in which she uses L2 Japanese, L3 Korean and L4 Mandarin (Chapter 6). Yian (L1: English, L2: Mandarin, L3: Japanese, L4: Korean), who has a Chinese background, imagined a multilingual vision, and her heritage language (Mandarin) had an important role in it. She was learning Korean in addition to Japanese and reported that she imagined a multilingual vision in which she speaks four languages interchangeably as a hotel clerk. Interestingly, Yian's multilingual vision is made up of English and three Asian languages (Mandarin, Japanese and Korean), which is the same combination as that of Laura, who has an English monolingual background. Therefore, it is possible that the combination of these Asian languages is likely to facilitate the construction of learners' ideal multilingual vision, partly because of the overlapping linguistic and cultural aspects and coherence as part of Asian identities. Nevertheless, Iseok (L1: Korean, L2: English, L3: Japanese, L4: Mandarin) and Luyue (L1: English, L2: Cantonese, L3: Japanese, L4: Mandarin, L5: Korean), who were also learning another Asian language in addition to Japanese at university, did not provide any evidence of their multilingual visions as a significant motivational force.

Considering these examples in terms of DST, the combination of these Asian languages may be one of the system parameters, which influence the coadaptation between the participants' motivational systems. That is, because of the parameter, ideal L2, L3, L4… self-systems within a learner can easily interact with each other, which facilitates the emergence of a new dynamic system at a higher level (*ideal multilingual self-system*). However, it is also possible that the emergence of the higher order dynamic system can be influenced by other internal and external conditions, such as the quality of the ideal L2 self-system and impact of mono/multicultural society. Importantly, multilingual visions of the above four informants (Oyeon, Junha, Laura and Yian) are generally stable and elaborate, which supports Henry's (2017: 554) argument that 'ideal multilingual self will create increased stability and cohesion within the multilingual identity system'. Thus, I argue that one's ideal multilingual self, which is made up of two or more languages, can have a wider and deeper attractor basin than one's ideal L2 self, which is comprised of a single language. Also, ideal multilingual self can be viewed as a *fixed attractor* to which multiple motivational systems are gravitated, contributing to the stability of the systems (see Hiver 2015).

Competition or coadaptation?

The concept of ideal multilingual self helps explain the complex nature of multiple motivations within a language learner. In the cases of two Australian learners (Emma and Diane) whose ideal French (L2) selves were negatively influenced by their ideal Japanese (L3) selves, the informants' L2 and L3 self-guides seemed to *compete* with each other. However, the cases of the four informants (Oyeon, Junha, Laura and Yian), who envisage their ideal multilingual selves, showed that their ideal L2 and L3 (and L4) selves appeared to dynamically interact with each other to generate more complex future self-guides. L2 motivation studies which focus on the relationship between different target languages (e.g. Csizér and Dörnyei 2005; Henry 2014; Csizér and Lukács 2010) have repeatedly claimed that different language-specific visions often compete with each other (see Chapter 2). The underlying assumption is that there is finite cognitive space to work on more than one language, or in Csizér and Dörnyei's (2005: 657) words, 'learners' limited language learning capacity', where one language wins and the other must lose. However, Ortega (2016: 60), citing Cook, questions the assumption from the perspective of *multi-competence* and claims as follows:

> Many, probably most, bilinguals develop unequal skills in their languages, as a natural result of what Grosjean (2008) calls the *complementarity* principle: they use different languages and combination of languages across different domains of life and social networks. This being so, a central preoccupation among bilingualism researchers is to understand the processes by which, within the bilingual user's total system, a language may weaken or strengthen overall, with respect to the other(s). The place of these concerns within the multi-competence perspective is questionable, as the metaphor of dominance may serve to reify

the idea of separate languages that, instead of interacting dynamically, compete (Vivian Cook, personal communication, July 18, 2014).

Therefore, in order to understand the relationship between ideal L2 and L3 (and L4 …) selves within a learner, it might be productive to interpret the relationship as a continuous interaction, or *coadaptation*, between a learner's L2 and L3 self-systems, which can trigger the emergence of a more complex dynamic system (ideal multilingual self). Different language-specific self-guides can coexist within a learner in the form of a multilingual vision, linked to a particular domain (or domains) of life. In this sense, *competition* between different L2 self-images, in which one language wins and the other loses, can be viewed as one of the forms of coadaptation (see also Henry 2017).

Signature dynamics of motivational trajectories

Signature dynamics in sustained motivational trajectory

Through DST analysis, ten Australian and four Korean informants were classified into the sustained motivational trajectory. The signature dynamics underlying the trajectory can be described as a strengthening of ideal L2 self-system through the coadaptation with other systems, such as L2 learning experience, and current L2 self. As Laura's case indicated, the participants were initially interested in Japanese language/culture. However, after moving from secondary school to university, the learners come to pay more attention to their future careers/plans and have L2 learning/use experiences that are more related to career (e.g. a business Japanese course, part-time jobs and volunteer). Positive L2 learning and use experiences at high school and university help enhance their current self-view as a Japanese user, which encourages them to seek out opportunities to use the language in the future.

Figure 7.1, which represents a part of the trajectory, shows that the participants' enhanced current L2 self and L2 experiences in class and outside of the classroom can be a sound basis for the upward revision of their ideal Japanese self. Because of the revision, there continues to exist a discrepancy between their current and ideal L2 selves, which sustains their motivation. This confirms the argument in psychology that individuals establish future self-guides on the basis of already developed current sense of self (Oyserman and Fryberg 2006). In the figure, the development of ideal and current self (in terms of skills and range of domains) is represented by straight lines, but in reality, neither the ideal nor the

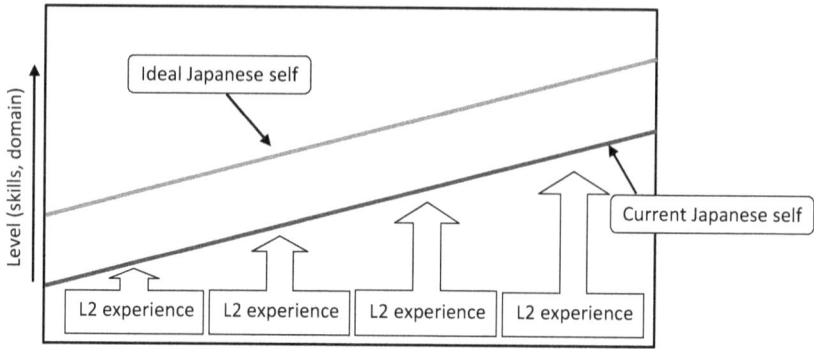

Figure 7.1 Development of ideal Japanese self in sustained motivational trajectory

current self develops smoothly. For example, learners' current self-image can be revised dramatically when significant events take place (e.g. achieving desired test score, having positive experiences while travelling in Japan), whereas it can be very stable when the events do not happen. Nevertheless, the evolution of ideal and current L2 selves is simply illustrated in the figure just for convenience of explanation.

From a DST perspective, an important initial condition of the participants' Japanese motivational system can be characterized as an attractor, *interest in Japanese language/culture*, which helps the development of their ideal and current Japanese self connected to the leisure domain. Their Japanese motivational system develops based on the coadapting relationship between L2 learning experience, ideal Japanese self and current L2 self. That is, the development of L2 learning experience as a dynamic system contributes to the development of current L2 self-system. The strengthened current L2 self-system pushes ideal Japanese self-system into a deeper attractor state. The strengthened ideal Japanese self-system, then, facilitates the further development of L2 learning experience, and so forth. Through the coadapting process, the larger L2 motivational system, in which ideal L2 self-system and L2 learning experience are embedded, comes to have a deeper basin of attractor.

Especially in the Australian context, after the informants entered university, demands for bilingual native speakers of English in Japan seemed to have a positive impact on the construction, or evolution, of their ideal Japanese selves. As de Bot (2016) claims, the link between the social and the psychological aspects of the individual can be explained through the interconnectedness of systems: the human cognitive system is embodied in the larger social system, and there is continuous interaction between the social and cognitive systems.

Further, DST assumes that the movement of a system is guided by system parameters (Hiver 2015). Thus, it is possible that a shift of the larger dynamic system at an institutional and life-phase level (i.e. transition from high school to university) contributed to propel the participants' Japanese motivational system into a new state, where career-related ideal Japanese self is an attractor. In this process, *demands for bilingual native speakers of English* plays a role as a system parameter, which had an increasing effect on the movement of their motivational systems.

Signature dynamics in waning motivational trajectory

However, three Australian and eight Korean informants were classified under the waning motivational trajectory. The underlying mechanism of the trajectory can be viewed as a motivational decline due to the achievement, or diminishment, of ideal L2 self. Similar to the sustained motivational trajectory, the participants' interest in Japanese language/culture can be characterized as the initial condition of their Japanese motivational system, which contributed to the construction of their ideal Japanese self (especially within the leisure domain). As they entered university and progressed through their courses, they came to place more importance on their future careers than on their intrinsic interests. However, unlike the first trajectory, their ideal Japanese selves were not revised upwardly, and for some participants they became less distinct. The participants in the waning trajectory, in general, had unsuccessful Japanese learning experiences and came to have less Japanese use experience than before, which does not seem to enhance their current Japanese self and promote their ideal Japanese self.

Here, there seem to be two patterns of negative development of their ideal Japanese self. Figure 7.2 represents Iseok's (Chapter 6) case, in which after the achievement of a learning goal, the ideal Japanese self stops further development. As the distance between ideal and current Japanese self diminishes, the ideal Japanese self comes to lose its motivational power. Figure 7.3 represents Minseop (Chapter 5), Cheonga (Chapter 5) and Scott's (Chapter 6) cases. Their ideal Japanese selves were initially linked to enjoying pop culture or travelling abroad. However, partly due to the difficulties of the study or their negative expectations to use Japanese for their careers, their ideal Japanese selves became vague, which is indicated in the figure as a dotted line. With the decreasing vividness, the motivational power of their ideal Japanese selves appeared to decline.

From a DST perspective, in Australia, Iseok and Scott's decreasing usage of Japanese in or outside of the classroom (and unsuccessful Japanese study in

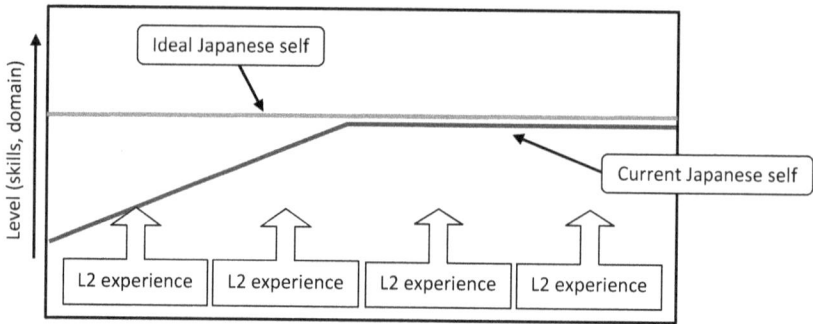

Figure 7.2 Development of ideal Japanese self in waning motivational trajectory (Type 1: Achievement of ideal Japanese self)

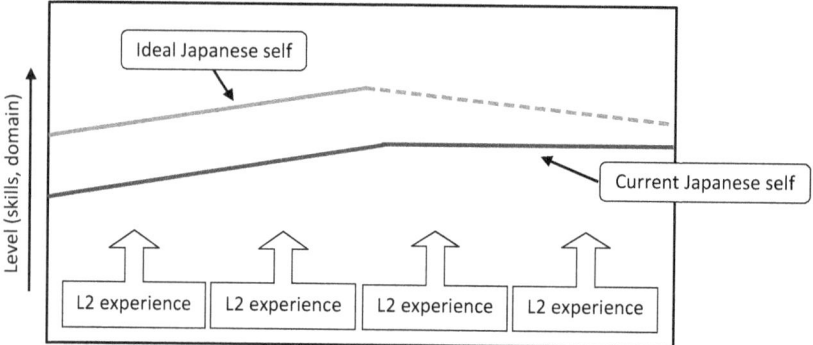

Figure 7.3 Development of ideal Japanese self in waning motivational trajectory (Type 2: Weakening of ideal Japanese self)

Scott's case) contributed to narrowing down the attractor basin of their Japanese motivational system. Another Australian informant, Shiyi, suffered from parental pressure not to pursue Japanese-related career paths, which also negatively influenced the development of her Japanese motivational system. In the Korean context, as the informants progressed in their degrees, many of them came under an institutional pressure to meet graduation requirements, and four stopped formal Japanese study. Also, *demands for English as a career language* appeared to further contribute to the lack of the Korean informants' long-term Japanese goals/visions. For many Korean participants, Japanese was not seen as a necessary or desirable component of their multilingual selves, at least within the career domain. In other words, both the weakening of the subsystem (ideal L2 self) and the increasing negative impact of the larger systems at a macro (institutional/social) level contribute to the weakening of the Korean informants' Japanese motivational system and thus the formation of waning motivational trajectory.

Practical implications

The current study carries some important implications for language education, more generally, and LOTE education, in particular. First of all, the concept of *domain of L2 self* implies that learner's L2 self, which is linked to particular domains of life, is also related to particular domain-specific types of L2. As Bakhtin (1986: 60) emphasizes, each domain of human activity, in which language is used, develops its own relatively stable types of utterances, called *speech genres*. Especially in the cases of LOTE learning, as the present study has demonstrated, learners are likely to envision their future self-guides, in which they are using or speaking particular speech genres of the target language used/spoken specifically in particular life domains (e.g. dramas, scientific research, business) in L2 community. Given that, vision-enhancing pedagogical approach based on the L2 Motivational Self System (cf. Hadfield and Dörnyei 2013; Dörnyei and Kubanyiova 2014) will have benefits from adapting the concept of domain of L2 self. For instance, when an L2 teacher knows the domains of life in which her/his students will use the L2 in the future, introducing and practicing the domain-specific speech genres of the language may help enhance the elaborateness of the students' ideal L2 selves connected to the domains.

Secondly, in the learning contexts where linguistic/cultural distance between individual's mother tongue and target language is large (e.g. Australia–Japan), support from the language teacher at an early stage of learning is vital. The data showed that some Australian participants were able to maintain their interest in Japanese language/culture and envisage their ideal self-images as users of the language thanks to the teachers' continuing support for their study. Particularly, language teachers need to understand their potential role in helping to foster an ideal self for each student. In addition, some Australian learners' learning experiences in Japan when in high school were found to be important sources for the construction of their actual and hoped-for self-representations as Japanese users. Therefore, in these contexts, study abroad and cultivation of opportunities to interact with local speakers of the target language should be more encouraged by schools from an early stage of L2 learning. For the contexts where the distance from target language/culture is small (e.g. Korea–Japan, UK–Germany), easiness to achieve a certain level of language proficiency might be an attractive aspect for many learners. However, if a learner focuses too much on attaining a short-term goal, her/his motivation may decrease after receiving the result, such as when she/he has achieved a desired test score. In these contexts, the importance of students' future self-guide, which is linked not only to the academic domain but also to various life domains, should be stressed (Nakamura 2015). Especially, the motivational impact of ideal L2 self-image which is linked to the leisure domain (e.g. enjoying pop culture) should be acknowledged, and where possible, classroom experiences should address this goal. Additionally, encouraging students to seek possible opportunities to communicate with people who speak the target language in and outside of the classroom may contribute to promote their ideal L2 self-concept which is connected to the interpersonal domain.

Through the comparative analysis between the sustained and waning motivational trajectories, the present study found that current L2 self, which is enhanced through positive L2 learning experience in and outside of the classroom, can be a sound basis of ideal L2 self. Especially in the Korean context, the participants' limited opportunities to use Japanese outside of the classroom as well as the institutional pressure to achieve required test scores seemed to negatively influence the establishment of their current identity as Japanese users. Lyons (2014) also says that testing occupies a considerable amount of Korean high school learners' focus and time, which prevents them from setting individual goals or formulating a vision of themselves. Hence, in this context, it is necessary to seek out the ways to promote their current Japanese selves through positive learning experiences. In the field of Japanese language education, Hosokawa (2002) proposed a pedagogical approach which focuses on learners' self-realization in the target language. Compared with the conventional teaching approaches that have principally aimed to develop learners' particular L2 skills, such as communicative competence, the approach aims to promote learners' identity through their self-expression and interaction with others in Japanese (Hosokawa 2002). For the learners to develop healthy L2 self-guides, this kind of approach might be particularly beneficial.

In addition, the current study, which examined learners' motivation across multiple languages, further suggests that the pedagogical approach needs to focus more on promoting learners' ideal multilingual self. From a multilingual perspective, Cook (2007) classified goals of language teaching into *external* goals that relate to actual second language use outside the classroom (e.g. communicative competence) and *internal* goals that relate to the students' mental development as individuals (e.g. linguistic/cultural awareness, cognitive flexibility, being better citizens). Based on the classification, the author claimed that language teaching should emphasize internal, not just external, educational goals that aim to promote learners' *linguistic multi-competence*, which refers to 'the overall system of a mind or a community that uses more than one language'

(Cook 2016: 2). Similarly, Leung and Scarino (2016) also proposed that the goals for language learning should encompass: (1) multilinguality as the fundamental orientation, (2) the formation and transformation of identities in and through language learning, (3) reflectivity and reflexivity in communication and learning to communicate. The L2 Motivational Self System brought about a new practical approach, which aims to promote learners' ideal self in a target language (e.g. Hadfield and Dörnyei 2013; Dörnyei and Kubanyiova 2014). However, it has paid little attention to the interrelationship between their ideal L2 and L3 (and L4) self-images and *internal* goals, such as the development of translingual/transcultural competence and cognitive flexibility. Therefore, I suggest that the vision-enhancing approach based on the L2 Motivational Self System should focus more on the development of learners' ideal multilingual self, in which they are able to interact across cultural boundaries, than the development of their ideal L2 self in a single target language (see also Ushioda 2017; Henry 2017).

In line with this view, in the contexts, where English is recognized as an essential language for one's future success (e.g. Korea, China), teachers of LOTEs should avail themselves of English for their teaching. That is, instead of trying to reduce the negative impact of English on their students' motivation for learning the language they teach, it might be more beneficial to consider how to promote their students' multilingual vision, in which they use both English and the target language (and other languages if any), to operate in a global society. In contrast, in the contexts where English is spoken as an L1 (e.g. Australia, the USA and the UK), it may be helpful for LOTE teachers to promote their students' ideal multilingual selves, in which they use both the target language and L1 English in particular domains of life. When the students learn two or more languages (e.g. Japanese, Korean and Mandarin) at the same time, it is advisable to support the simultaneous learning to promote their multilingual visions. Especially in Australia, where many students have Asian backgrounds, it is wise to encourage learning about other languages and cultures, particularly heritage languages. These efforts may promote not only the students' wider Asian literacy and linguistic multi-competence but also their ideal multilingual self.

Suggestions for future research

This study showed that cross-linguistic study might allow us to investigate L2 motivation as well as the developmental process of language-specific future selves, more deeply than monolingual analysis does. Also, multiple-case study was shown to be useful to identify the dynamic relationship between context and L2 motivation. However, there is a need for further investigation of issues raised in this study to be undertaken. Because of the absence of in-depth studies of Japanese language learners' motivation from an L2 self perspective, the present study was specifically designed to generate new context-sensitive insights about the dynamic nature of the construct. Consequently, this meant that the research needed to create boundaries in order to gain depth of understandings. As the situation in other Korean and Australian universities was not investigated in this study, it is difficult to provide a sufficient basis for generalization. Results may not be representative of the populations of all universities in Korea and Australia. Also, since the initial focus of attention was on the development of learners' L2 self, as well as L2 motivation, the dynamic changes of the other motivational components, such as their interest in target language/culture, were not investigated in as much depth. This restricted the ability to understand the whole picture of their L2 motivational trajectory. Methodologically, participants were not randomly selected, but were self-selected and thus probably included more highly motivated learners than the average, which might reduce the external validity of the findings. A random sample of students in general would have uncovered a more accurate picture of Japanese learners' motivation in each context. However, the strength of this study is that it establishes a point of reference from which others can investigate the dynamics of L2 learners' motivation in their own institutions. Clearly, further research is needed to explore the dynamics of Japanese language learners' motivation situated in and across a range of settings and contexts (e.g. with a range of proficiency levels and ages of learners, in Japanese as a second language context, in informal/formal setting) and involving a variety of foreign languages.

In addition, the participants' responses might have been affected by the interaction with the researcher (Mann 2011, 2016). For example, responses might have been influenced by social desirability, or a possible Hawthorne effect (Dörnyei 2007: 53). That is, participants might have worked harder or answered positively because they realized that they were research participants. Also, the interaction between the researcher and the participants in the interviews might influence the establishment of their goals or the construction of their ideal L2 selves. In her response to the follow-up questions on the second interview, Oyeon commented by email as follows:

こう申してしまうと少し恥ずかしいですが、私はインタビューを受けるまで自分がどうして日本語の勉強をしているかについて考

えることもなく、目的なく日本語の勉強自体が楽しくて勉強して
いるだけでした。でもA先生から色んな質問をされながらそれに
答えているうちに、今までとは違って自分にとって日本語の勉強
は何なのか、そして … 何年前から勉強してきた日本語を未来、
どのように使うべきか、将来、どんな職業に就いたら日本語を
より生かせるかについて前よりじっくり考えるようになりました。

[To my shame, before I attended the interview, I had studied Japanese without thinking about the reason or purpose to study it. I just studied it because the study itself was interesting. However, through answering to a variety of questions you asked, I came to consider more about what is the significance of studying Japanese for me … how to use the language that I had studied for years in the future, and what kind of career should I pursue to make better use of the language.]

The development of the participants' motivation for learning Japanese might be partly influenced by the process of participation in this study. However, this example also tells us the pedagogical benefits of interviewing and discussing learners' future L2-related goals. That is, discussion about the students' L2 goals or L2-related future plans can be a useful approach which helps generate and crystallize their ideal L2 selves.

Among the findings of this study, there are four areas that stand out as directions for future research. First of all, the current study found that the development of one's ideal L2 self is closely related to the development of one's current L2 self-image, or L2 identity. Although researchers started to combine different perspectives on the *self* to gain a more comprehensible picture of the self in second language acquisition (Mercer and Williams 2014), the complex relationship between current and ideal L2 selves has not been adequately investigated yet. Therefore, it requires a more detailed investigation than was carried out here. Secondly, this study revealed that the impact of Global English on motivation for learning additional languages varies depending on the social/linguistic context. Thus, both impacts of English as an L1 and as an L2 on motivation for learning additional languages would be an interesting area of research. Thirdly, the qualitative analysis uncovered that examining L2 self in isolation misses important aspects of how individuals see themselves as multilingual speakers, and therefore it is suggested that learners' *ideal multilingual self* is an important motivational construct. Clearly, the concept of ideal multilingual self has significant motivational implications, which requires further investigation. Finally, the concept of domain of L2 self has potentially a great deal to offer to extend our knowledge of motivation across multiple languages and thus would be a promising research area.

Concluding remarks

Through the comparisons between different target languages and contexts, the present study contributed to understanding Japanese language learners' motivation in two countries with different social and academic contexts, and in relation to their multilingual self-view. Drawing on Dörnyei's (2005) L2 Motivational Self System, the concept of domain of possible selves and DST, this study uncovered how Japanese language learners' future self-guides as bi/multilingual users and other motivational components are related – how these factors influence their engagement in the learning. It also revealed the motivational relationships between different languages the learners possess and the role of English (as an L1 and as an L2) in shaping the way in which learners engage with Japanese. To be sure, many of the motivational changes identified here would have surfaced even if the data had been analyzed without the benefit of a DST lens. However, as dynamic systems are considered to be in constant interaction with other systems and the contexts in which they are embedded, sensitivity to these interactions enabled me to explain how motivational fluctuations were triggered and how the changes of motivational constructs took place. Also, adopting the approach together with the concept of domain of L2 self made it possible to gain profound insights into how learner's different language-specific visions are related.

As Markus and Nurius (1986: 955) point out, 'development can be seen as a process of acquiring and then achieving or resisting certain possible selves'. People seek to maintain, revise and expand their future self-concepts continuously throughout different stages of their lives. Thus, the link between future L2 self-guide and L2 motivation, which has been indicated by SLA researchers to date, can be viewed as an integral part of human development. This link needs to be extended according to the outcomes of this study to accommodate multilingual perspectives. Studying multilingual vision will promote deeper understanding of language learning as human development in an era of globalization and multilingualism.

Appendix 1(a)

First round interview questions (Australian version)

1. What language or languages do you and your family use at home?
   - Who speaks it?
   - How often?
   - Did your parents encourage you to use the language?

2. (If the language was compulsory at school)
   - For how long was it compulsory?
   - Why did you decide to continue with () after that?

   (If the language was not compulsory)
   - Why did you choose to study () at the beginning?
   - Why did you continue to study () until (depends on the experience)?

3. Please describe your learning experience of ().
4. Did you have any chance to use () outside of the classroom?
   - With whom?
   - How often?

   (If he/she does not mention pop culture)
   - How about reading *manga* or listening to music or watching movies of ()?

5. At that time, did you think you might use the language in the future?
   - If so, in what ways?

6. At that time, did your parents, teachers and friends encourage (or discourage) you to study ()?
   - Why did they encourage (or discourage) you?

7. Thinking back to the commencement of your study of () at the university, why did you decide to study ()?
8. Why did you decide to continue with () this semester?
9. Please describe your learning experience of () at the university.
10. How much time and effort do you put into studying () now?
11. Do you have any chance to use () outside of the classroom?

    - With whom?
    - How often?

    (If he/she does not mention pop culture)

    - How about reading *manga* or listening to music or watching movies of ()?

12. (If he/she has experience of visiting foreign countries)

    - What did you do there?
    - Did you have any chance to use ()?
    - Did you have different attitudes after visiting the country?
    - Do you want to visit there again? Why?

    (If he/she does not have experience of visiting)

    - Do you want to visit the country?
    - If so, why?

13. Do you have any significant events (or people) in your learning history of ()?
14. (If the L2 was not learnt at school or university)

    Please describe your learning experience of () at home.

15. How do you feel about your ability to communicate in ()?
16. When you think about yourself as a () learner or user, how confident are you?

    - When do you feel confidence (or lack of confidence)?
    - What affects your confidence as a () speaker/writer?

17. (If studying the L2 now) What are your goals of studying ()?
18. What do you want to do after you graduate?
19. (If only Japanese) When you think of your future career, do you imagine yourself using Japanese or knowledge gained through Japanese learning?

- In what situations?
- How?

(For trilingual students) When you think of your future career, what languages do you think you might use?

- In what situations?
- How?

20. (If only Japanese) When you think of your future relationship with your family members or friends, do you imagine yourself using Japanese?

    - In what situations?
    - How?

    (For trilingual students) When you think of your future relationship with your family members or friends, what languages do you think you might use?

    - In what situations?
    - How?

21. (If only Japanese) When you think of leisure activities in your future life, do you imagine yourself using Japanese?

    - In what situations?
    - How?

    (For trilingual students) When you think of your future leisure activities, what languages do you think you might use?

    - In what situations?
    - How?

22. How long do you think you will continue to study Japanese?

    - Why do you think so?
    - (If continue after graduation) Where? How?

23. Is there anything else you would like to add?

Appendix 1(b)

First round interview questions (Korean version)

1. 당신과 당신 가족이 집에서 사용하는 언어(들)는 무엇입니까?
   - 누가 사용합니까?
   - 얼마나 자주 사용합니까?
   - 당신의 부모님은 당신이 그 언어를 사용하는 것을 격려합니까?

2. (만일 해당 언어가 학교에서 필수 과목이었다면)
   - 얼마나 오랜 기간 필수 과목이었습니까?
   - 당신은 왜 그 후에도 ()를 계속해서 공부기로 결심하였습니까?

   (만일 해당 언어가 학교에서 필수 과목이 아니었다면)
   - 당신은 초기에 왜 ()를 선택하였습니까?
   - 당신은 왜 ()를 () 까지 계속해서 공부하였습니까?

3. 당신의 ()를 학습한 경험을 서술하시오.
4. 당신은 교실 밖에서 ()를 사용할 기회가 있습니까?
   - 누구와?
   - 얼마나 자주?

   (만일, 학생이 대중문화를 언급하지 않는다면)
   - (어)만화를 읽거나, 음악을 듣거나, 영화를 보기도 했었습니까?

5. 그 때 당시, 당신은 향후에 당신이 그 언어를 사용하게 될 거라는 생각을 했었습니까?
   - 만일 그렇다면, 어떤 식으로?

6. 그 때 당시, 당신의 부모님이나 선생님, 혹은 친구들이 당신이 ()를 공부하는 것을 격려하거나 (혹은, 말린다거나) 했었습니까?

Appendix 1(b)

- 그들은 왜 격려하거나(혹은, 말린다거나) 했었습니까?

7. 당신이 대학에서 ()를 공부한 초기로 돌아가 생각해 봅시다. 당신은 왜 ()를 공부하기로 결심했었습니까?
8. 당신은 왜 해당학기에 () 를 계속 하기로 결심했습니까?
9. 대학에서 ()를 학습한 경험에 대해 서술하시오.
10. 당신은 현재 ()를 공부하는데, 얼마나 많은 시간과 노력을 하고 있습니까?
11. 당신은 교실 밖에서 ()를 사용할 기회가 있습니까?

    - 누구와?
    - 얼마나 자주?

    (만일, 학생이 대중문화를 언급하지 않는다면)

    - (어)만화를 읽거나, 음악을 듣거나, 영화를 보기도 했었습니까?

12. (만일 외국에 방문한 경험이 있다면)

    - 그 나라에서 무엇을 하였습니까?
    - 그 나라에서 ()을 사용할 기회가 있었습니까?
    - 그 나라를 방문한 후에 당신의 태도가 달라졌습니까?
    - 그 나라를 다시 방문하고 싶습니까? 왜입니까?

    (만일 외국에 방문한 경험이 없다면)

    - 외국에 방문하길 원합니까?
    - 만일 그렇다면, 왜입니까?

13. 당신의 () 학습역사에 있어서 어떤 의미 있는 사건(혹은, 인물들)이 있습니까?
14. (만일 당신이 학교 혹은, 대학에서 제2언어를 배우지 않았다면)

    집에서()를 학습한 경험을 서술하시오.

15. ()로 의사소통을 하는 당신의 능력에 대해 어떻게 느끼고 있습니까?
16. 당신을 ()학습자 혹은 사용자로서 생각할 때, 얼마나 자신감을 느낍니까?

    - 언제 자신감을 느낍니까? (혹은, 언제 자신감이 부족함을 느낍니까?)
    - () 사용자로서 당신의 자신감은 어떤 영향을 끼칩니까?

17. (현재 제2언어를 배우고 있다면) 당신의 ()학습에 대한 목표는 무엇입니까?

18. 졸업 후에 무엇을 하기를 희망합니까?
19. (오직 일본어 학습자) 당신의 향후 경력에 대해 생각할 때, 당신은 일본어 학습을 통해서 배운 지식이나 일본어를 사용하는 자신을 상상합니까?

    - 어떤 상황들에서?
    - 어떻게?

    (3개국어이상 학습경험자) 당신의 향후 경력에 대해 생각할 때, 당신은 어떤 언어를 사용할 것이라고 생각합니까?

    - 어떤 상황들에서?
    - 어떻게?

20. (오직 일본어 학습자) 당신의 향후 가족과의 관계, 혹은 친구와의 관계에 대해 생각할 때, 일본어를 사용하는 자신을 상상합니까?

    - 어떤 상황들에서?
    - 어떻게?

    (3개국어이상 학습경험자) 당신의 향후 가족과의 관계, 혹은 친구와의 관계에 대해 생각할 때, 당신은 어떤 언어를 사용할 것이라고 생각합니까?

    - 어떤 상황에서?
    - 어떻게?

21. (오직 일본어 학습자) 당신의 향후 삶의 여가활동에 대해 생각할 때, 일본어를 사용하는 자신을 상상합니까?

    - 어떤 상황들에서?
    - 어떻게?

    (3개국어이상 학습경험자) 당신의 향후 삶의 여가활동에 대해 생각할 때 당신은 어떤 언어를 사용할 것이라고 생각합니까?

    - 어떤 상황들에서?
    - 어떻게?

22. 당신은 얼마나 오래 일본어 학습을 지속할 생각입니까?

    - 왜 그럴려고 생각합니까?
    - (만일 졸업 후에 계속 하려고 한다면) 어디에서? 어떻게?

23. 보충하고 싶은 것이 있습니까? (더 하고 싶은 이야기가 있습니까?)

Appendix 2(a)

Second round interview questions (Australian version)

1. (If studying the L2 now) Please describe your learning experience of () in this seven-month period.
2. Please describe how you used () outside of the classroom in this period.
3. Were there any significant events relating to () in this period?
   - If yes, why significant for you?
4. How do you feel about your ability to communicate in ()?
   - Has this changed over the seven-month period?
   - If so, what has affected the change?
5. When you think about yourself as a () learner or user, how confident are you?
   - Has this changed over the period?
   - If so, what has affected the change?
6. (If studying the L2 now) What are your goals of studying ()?
   - Has this changed over the period?
   - If so, what has affected the change?
7. What do you want to do after you graduate?
   - Has this changed over the period?
   - If so, what has affected the change?
8. (If only Japanese) When you think of your future career, do you imagine yourself using Japanese or knowledge gained through Japanese learning?
   - In what situations?
   - (If changed) Why has it changed?

(For trilingual students) When you think of your future career, what languages do you think you might use?

- In what situations?
- (If changed) Why has it changed?

9. (If only Japanese) When you think of your future relationship with your family members or friends, do you imagine yourself using Japanese?

    - In what situations?
    - (If changed) Why has it changed?

    (For trilingual students) When you think of your future relationship with your family members or friends, what languages do you think you might use?

    - In what situations?
    - (If changed) Why has it changed?

10. (If only Japanese) When you think of leisure activities in your future life, do you imagine yourself using Japanese?

    - In what situations?
    - (If changed) Why has it changed?

    (For trilingual students) When you think of your future leisure activities, what languages do you think you might use?

    - In what situations?
    - (If changed) Why has it changed?

11. How long do you think you will continue to study Japanese?

    - (If changed) Why has it changed?

12. How would you rate your motivation for studying Japanese these seven months?
13. Is there anything else you would like to add?

Appendix 2(b)

Second round interview questions (Korean version)

1. (현재 제2언어를 배우고 있다면) 최근 8개월 사이에 학습 중인 ()의 학습경험에 대해 서술하시오.
2. 이 기간안에 ()를 교실 밖에서 어떻게 사용했는지 서술하시오.
3. 이 기간안에 ()와 관련된 어떠한 중요한 사건이 있었습니까?
   - 만일 있었다면, 그 일이 당신에게 있어서 왜 중요합니까?
4. ()로 의사소통을 하는 당신의 능력에 대해 어떻게 느끼고 있습니까?
   - 8개월 사이에 당신의 능력에 변화가 있었습니까?
   - 만일 그렇다면, 무엇이 그 변화에 영향을 끼쳤습니까?
5. 당신을 ()학습자 혹은 사용자로서 생각할 때, 얼마나 자신감을 느낍니까?
   - 이 기간 동안 이 자신감이 변했습니까?
   - 만일 그렇다면, 무엇이 그 변화에 영향을 끼쳤습니까?
6. (현재 제2언어를 배우고 있다면) 당신의 ()학습에 대한 목표는 무엇입니까?
   - 이 기간 동안 당신의 학습목표가 변했습니까?
   - 만일 그렇다면, 무엇이 그 변화에 영향을 끼쳤습니까?
7. 졸업 후에 무엇을 하기를 희망합니까?
   - 이 기간 동안 당신의 희망이 변했습니까?
   - 만일 그렇다면, 무엇이 그 변화에 영향을 끼쳤습니까?
8. (오직 일본어 학습자) 당신의 향후 경력에 대해 생각할 때, 당신은 일본어 학습을 통해서 배운 지식이나 일본어를 사용하는 자신을 상상합니까?

- 어떤 상황들에서?
- (만일 변했다면) 왜 변했습니까?

(3개국어이상 학습경험자) 당신의 향후 경력에 대해 생각할 때, 당신은 어떤 언어를 사용할 것이라고 생각합니까?

- 어떤 상황들에서?
- (만일 변했다면) 왜 변했습니까?

9. (오직 일본어 학습자) 당신의 향후 가족과의 관계, 혹은 친구와의 관계에 대해 생각할 때, 일본어를 사용하는 자신을 상상합니까?

- 어떤 상황들에서?
- (만일 변했다면) 왜 변했습니까?

(3개국어이상 학습경험자) 당신의 향후 가족과의 관계, 혹은 친구와의 관계에 대해 생각할 때, 당신은 어떤 언어를 사용할 것이라고 생각합니까?

- 어떤 상황에서?
- (만일 변했다면) 왜 변했습니까?

10. (오직 일본어 학습경험자) 당신의 향후 삶의 여가활동에 대해 생각할 때,

일본어를 사용하는 자신을 상상합니까?

- 어떤 상황들에서?
- (만일 변했다면) 왜 변했습니까?

(3개국어이상 학습경험자) 당신의 향후 삶의 여가활동에 대해 생각할 때 당신은 어떤 언어를 사용할 것이라고 생각합니까?

- 어떤 상황들에서?
- (만일 변했다면) 왜 변했습니까?

11. 당신은 얼마나 오래 일본어 학습을 지속할 생각입니까?

- (만일 변했다면) 왜 변했습니까?

12. (10월부터 5월까지의) 7개월간 당신의 일본어 학습에 대한 동기를 어떻게 평가하겠습니까?
13. 보충하고 싶은 것이 있습니까? (더 하고 싶은 이야기가 있습니까?)

References

Bakhtin, M. M. (1986), *Speech Genres and Other Late Essays*, Austin: University of Texas Press.
Block, D. (2006), *Multilingual Identities in a Global City: London Stories*, London: Palgrave Macmillan.
Boo, Z., Z. Dörnyei and S. Ryan (2015), 'L2 Motivation Research 2005–2014: Understanding a Publication Surge and a Changing Landscape', *System*, 55: 145–57.
Bourdieu, P. and J. C. Passeron (1990), *Reproduction in Education, Society and Culture*, London: Newbury Park.
Buasaengtham, A. and M. Yoshinaga (2015), 'ライフストーリーから見られた非漢字圏日本語学習者の漢字学習への動機づけ：L2 Motivational Self Systemの観点から', 多文化社会と留学生交流, 19: 13–34.
Cenoz, J., B. Hufeisen and U. Jessner (2001), *Cross-linguistic Influence in Third Language Acquisition: Psycholinguistic Perspectives*, Bristol: Multilingual Matters.
Clyne, M. (2007), 'Are We Making Difference? On the Social Responsibility and Impact of the Linguist/Applied Linguist in Australia', *Australian Review of Applied Linguistics*, 30 (1): 3.1–3.14.
Cook, V. (2007), 'The Goals of ELT: Reproducing Native-Speakers or Promoting Multicompetence Among Second Language Users?' in J. Cummins and C. Davison (eds), *International Handbook of English Language Teaching*, 237–48, Dordrecht: Kluwer.
Cook, V. (2016), 'Premises of Multi-Competence', in V. Cook and W. Li (eds), *The Cambridge Handbook of Linguistic Multicompetence*, 1–25, Cambridge: Cambridge University Press.
Cross, S. E. and J. S. Gore (2003), 'Cultural Models of the Self', in M. R. Leary and J. P. Tangney (eds), *Handbook of Self and Identity*, 536–64, New York: Guilford Press.
Crowe, E. and E. T. Higgins (1997), 'Regulatory Focus and Strategic Inclinations: Promotion and Prevention in Decision-Making', *Organizational Behavior and Human Decision Processes*, 69 (2): 117–32.
Csizér, K. and Z. Dörnyei (2005), 'Language Learners' Motivational Profiles and Their Motivated Learning Behaviour', *Language Learning*, 55 (4): 613–59.
Csizér, K. and J. Kormos (2009), 'Learning Experiences, Selves and Motivated Learning Behaviour: A Comparative Analysis of Structural Models for Hungarian Secondary and University Learners of English', in Z. Dörnyei and E. Ushioda (eds), *Motivation, Language Identity and the L2 Self*, 98–119, Bristol: Multilingual Matters.

Csizér, K., J. Kormos and A. Sarkadi (2010), 'The Dynamics of Language Learning Attitudes and Motivation: Lessons from an Interview Study of Dyslexic Language Learners', *The Modern Language Journal*, 94: 470–87.

Csizér, K. and G. Lukács (2010), 'The Comparative Analysis of Motivation, Attitudes and Selves: The Case of English and German in Hungary', *System*, 38 (1): 1–13.

De Bot, K. (2016), 'Multi-Competence and Dynamic/Complex Systems', in V. Cook and W. Li (eds), *The Cambridge Handbook of Linguistic Multicompetence*, 1–25, Cambridge: Cambridge University Press.

De Bot, K., W. Lowie and M. Verspoor (2007), 'A Dynamic Systems Theory Approach to Second Language Acquisition', *Bilingualism: Language and Cognition*, 10 (1): 7–21.

Djafri, F. (2016), 'A Study on the Motivational Change of Japanese Learning in Higher Educational Institution: Narratives of Indonesian Japanese Learners', *Transcommunication*, 3 (2): 211–31.

Dörnyei, Z. (2005), *The Psychology of the Language Learner: Individual Differences in Second Language Acquisition*, Mahwah, NJ: Lawrence Erlbaum.

Dörnyei, Z. (2009), 'The L2 Motivational Self System', in Z. Dörnyei and E. Ushioda (eds), *Motivation, Language Identity and the L2 Self*, 9–42, Bristol: Multilingual Matters.

Dörnyei, Z. (2014), 'Researching Complex Dynamic Systems: "Retrodictive Qualitative Modelling" in the Language Classroom', *Language Teaching*, 47 (1): 80–91.

Dörnyei, Z. and A. H. Al-Hoorie (2017), 'The Motivational Foundation of Learning Languages Other Than Global English: Theoretical Issues and Research Directions. L2 Motivation and Multilingual Identities', *The Modern Language Journal*, 101 (3): 455–68.

Dörnyei, Z. and L. Chan (2013), 'Motivation and Vision: An Analysis of Future L2 Self Images, Sensory Styles, and Imagery Capacity Across Two Target Languages', *Language Learning*, 63 (3): 437–62.

Dörnyei, Z. and R. Clément (2001), 'Motivational Characteristics of Learning Different Target Languages: Results of a Nationwide Survey', *Motivation and Second Language Acquisition*, 23: 399–432.

Dörnyei, Z. and K. Csizér (2002), 'Some Dynamics of Language Attitudes and Motivation: Results of a Nationwide Survey', *Applied Linguistics*, 23: 421–62.

Dörnyei, Z. and M. Kubanyiova (2014), *Motivating Learners, Motivating Teachers: Building Vision in the Language Classroom*, Cambridge: Cambridge University Press.

Dörnyei, Z., P. D. MacIntyre and A. Henry (2015), *Motivational Dynamics in Language Learning*, Bristol: Multilingual Matters.

Dörnyei, Z. and E. Ushioda (2009), *Motivation, Language Identity and the L2 Self*, Bristol: Multilingual Matters.

Dörnyei, Z. and E. Ushioda (2011), *Teaching and Researching Motivation*, 2nd edn, Harlow: Pearson Education.

Downes, W. (1984), *Language and Society*, Bungay: Fontana.

Dunkel, C. S., D. Kelts and B. Coon (2006), 'Possible Selves as Mechanisms of Change in Therapy', in C. Dunkel and J. Kerpelman (eds), *Possible Selves: Theory, Research and Applications*, 187–204, New York: Nova Science Publishers.

Fishman, J. A. (1972), *Language in Sociocultural Change*, Stanford: Stanford University Press.

Gardner, R. C. (1985), *Social Psychology and Second Language Learning: The Role of Attitudes and Motivation*, London: Edward Arnold.

Gardner, R. C. (2001), 'Integrative Motivation and Second Language Acquisition', in Z. Dörnyei and R. Schmidt (eds), *Motivation and Second Language Acquisition*, 1–20, Honolulu: University of Hawaii Press.

Gardner, R. C. and W. E. Lambert (1959), 'Motivational Variables in Second Language Acquisition', *Canadian Journal of Psychology*, 13: 266–72.

Gardner, R. C. and W. E. Lambert (1972), *Attitudes and Motivation in Second Language Learning*, Rowley, MA: Newbury House.

Grosjean, F. (2008), *Studying Bilinguals*, Oxford: Oxford University Press.

Grosjean, F. (2010), *Bilingual: Life and Reality*, Cambridge: Harvard University Press.

Gumperz, J. J. (1972), *Directions in Sociolinguistics: The Ethnography of Communication*, New York: Holt, Rinehart and Winston.

Guo, J. and J. Quan (2006), '中国人大学生の日本語学習の動機づけについて', 新潟大学国際センター紀要, 2: 118–28.

Hadfield, J. and Z. Dörnyei (2013), *Motivating Learning*, Harlow: Longman.

Harada, T. (2010), '留学経験は学習動機にいかに関わっているか:「自己決定理論」に拠る「甲南大学 Year in Japan プログラム留学生」の留学と日本語学習の動機の変化', *言語と文化*, 12: 151–71.

Henry, A. (2010), 'Contexts of Possibilities in Simultaneous Language Learning: Using the L2 Motivational Self System to Assess the Impact of Global English', *Journal of Multilingual and Multicultural Development*, 31: 149–62.

Henry, A. (2011), 'Examining the Impact of L2 English on L3 Selves: A Case Study', *International Journal of Multilingualism*, 8: 235–55.

Henry, A. (2012), *L3 Motivation*, Göteborg, Sweden: Göteborgs Universitet.

Henry, A. (2014), 'The Motivational Effects of Crosslinguistic Awareness: Developing Third Language Pedagogies to Address the Negative Impact of the L2 on the L3 Self-Concept', *Innovation in Language Learning and Teaching*, 8 (1): 1–19.

Henry, A. (2015), 'The Dynamics of L3 Motivation: A Longitudinal Interview/Observation-Based Study', in Z. Dörnyei, P. MacIntyre and A. Henry (eds), *Motivational Dynamics in Language Learning*, 315–42, Bristol: Multilingual Matters.

Henry, A. (2017), 'L2 Motivation and Multilingual Identities', *The Modern Language Journal*, 101 (3): 548–65.

Herdina, P. and U. Jessner (2002), *A Dynamic Model of Multilingualism: Perspectives of Change in Psycholinguistics*, Bristol: Multilingual Matters.

Higgins, E. T. (1987), 'Self-Discrepancy: A Theory Relating Self and Affect', *Psychological Review*, 94: 319–40.

Higgins, E. T., R. Klein and T. Strauman (1985), 'Self-Concept Discrepancy Theory: A Psychological Model for Distinguishing Among Different Aspects of Depression and Anxiety', *Social Cognition*, 3 (1): 51–76.

Hiver, P. (2015), 'Attractor States', in Z. Dörnyei, P. MacIntyre and A. Henry (eds), *Motivational Dynamics in Language Learning*, 20–28, Bristol: Multilingual Matters.

Hosokawa, H. (2002), 日本語教育は何をめざすか—言語文化活動の理論と実践, Tokyo: Akashishoten.

Hoyle, R. H. and M. R. Sherrill (2006), 'Future Orientation in the Self-System: Possible Selves, Self-Regulation, and Behavior', *Journal of Personality*, 74 (6): 1673–96.

Huang, H. T., C. C. Hsu and S. W. Chen (2015), 'Identification with Social Role Obligations, Possible Selves, and L2 Motivation in Foreign Language Learning', *System*, 51: 28–38.

Irie, K. and D. R. Brewster (2015), 'Investing in Experiential Capital: Self-Efficacy, Imagination and Development of Ideal L2 Selves', in K. Csizér and M. Magid (eds), *The Impact of Self-Concept on Language Learning*, 171–88, Bristol: Multilingual Matters.

Irie, K. and S. Ryan (2015), 'Study Abroad and the Dynamics of Change in Learner L2 Self-Concept', in Z. Dörnyei, P. MacIntyre and A. Henry (eds), *Motivational Dynamics in Language Learning*, 343–66, Bristol: Multilingual Matters.

The Japan Foundation. (2017), 'Japanese-Language Education Overseas [Language]: Survey Report on Japanese-Language Education Abroad 2015', *The Japan Foundation*. Available online: https://www.jpf.go.jp/e/project/japanese/survey/result/survey15.html (accessed 20 August 2018).

Jessner, U. (2008a), 'Teaching Third Languages: Findings, Trends and Challenges', *Language Teaching*, 41 (1): 15–56.

Jessner, U. (2008b), 'A DST Model of Multilingualism and the Role of Metalinguistic Awareness', *The Modern Language Journal*, 92 (2): 270–83.

Kanno, Y. (2003), *Negotiating Bilingual and Bicultural Identities: Japanese Returnees Betwixt Two Worlds*, Mahwah, NJ: Lawrence Erlbaum Associates.

Kim, T.-Y. (2009), 'The Sociocultural Interface between Ideal Self and Ought-To Self: A Case Study of Two Korean Students' ESL Motivation', in Z. Dörnyei and E. Ushioda (eds), *Motivation, Language Identity and the L2 Self*, 274–94, Bristol: Multilingual Matters.

Kormos, J., T. Kiddle and K. Csizér (2011), 'Systems of Goals, Attitudes, and Self-Related Beliefs in Second-Language-Learning Motivation', *Applied Linguistics*, 32: 495–516.

Kurata, N. (2004), 'Communication Networks of Japanese Language Learners in Their Home Country', *Journal of Asian Pacific Communication*, 14 (1): 153–79.

Lamb, M. (2009), 'Situating the L2 Self: Two Indonesian School Learners of English', in Z. Dörnyei and E. Ushioda (eds), *Motivation, Language Identity and the L2 Self*, 229–47, Bristol: Multilingual Matters.

Lanvers, U. (2016), 'On the Predicaments of the English L1 Language Learner: A Conceptual Article', *International Journal of Applied Linguistics*, 26 (2): 147–67.

Larsen-Freeman, D. (2015), 'Ten "Lessons" from Complex Dynamic Systems Theory: What Is on Offer', in Z. Dörnyei, P. MacIntyre and A. Henry (eds), *Motivational Dynamics in Language Learning*, 11–19, Bristol: Multilingual Matters.

Larsen-Freeman, D. and L. Cameron (2008), 'Research Methodology on Language Development from a Complex Systems Perspective', *The Modern Language Journal*, 92 (2): 200–13.

LASP (Learned Academies Special Projects) (2007), *Beginners' LOTE (Languages Other than English) in Australian Universities: an Audit Survey and Analysis: Report to the Council of the Australian Academy of the Humanities*, Canberra: The Australian Academy of the Humanities.

LASP (Learned Academies Special Projects) (2009), *An Analysis of Retention Strategies and Technology Enhanced Learning in Beginners' Languages other than English (LOTE) at Australian Universities*, Canberra: The Australian Academy of the Humanities.

Leary, M. R. and J. P. Tangney (2003), *Handbook of Self and Identity*, New York: The Guilford Press.

Lee, S. H. (2003), '第2言語および外国語としての日本語学習者における動機づけの比較: 韓国人日本語学習者を対象として', *日本語教育論集*, 13: 75–92.

Leung, C. and A. Scarino (2016), 'Reconceptualizing the Nature of Goals and Outcomes in Language/s Education', *The Modern Language Journal*, 100 (Supplement 2016): 81–95.

Lo Bianco, J. (1987), *National Policy on Languages*, Canberra: Australian Government Publishing Service.

Lyons, D. (2014), 'The L2 Self-Concept in Second Language Learning Motivation: A Longitudinal Study of Korean University Students', *The Impact of Self-Concept on Language Learning*, 108–30, Bristol: Multilingual Matters.

MacIntyre, P. D., S. P. MacKinnon and R. Clément (2009), 'The Baby, the Bathwater, and the Future of Language Learning Motivation Research', in Z. Dörnyei and E. Ushioda (eds), *Motivation, Language Identity and the L2 Self*, 43–65, Bristol: Multilingual Matters.

Mann, S. M. (2011), 'A Critical Review of Qualitative Interviews in Applied Linguistics', *Applied Linguistics*, 32 (1): 6–24.

Mann, S. M. (2016), *The Research Interview: Reflective Practice and Reflexivity in the Research Process*, Basingstoke: Palgrave Macmillan.

Markus, H. and P. Nurius (1986), 'Possible Selves', *American Psychologist*, 41: 954–69.

Markus, H. and A. Ruvolo (1989), 'Possible Selves: Personalized Representations of Goals', in L. A. Pervin (ed.), *Goal Concepts in Personality and Social Psychology*, 211–42, Hillsdale, NJ: Lawrence Erlbaum.

Marsh, H. W., B. M. Byrne and R. Shavelson (1988), 'A Multifaceted Academic Self-Concept: Its Hierarchical Structure and Its Relation to Academic Achievement', *Journal of Educational Psychology*, 80 (3): 366–80.

Marsh, H. W., U. Trautwein., O. Lüdtke., O. Köller and J. Baumert (2006), 'Integration of Multidimensional Self-Concept and Core Personality Constructs: Construct Validation and Relations to Well-Being and Achievement', *Journal of Personality*, 74 (2): 403–456.

Matsumoto, M. (2009), Persistence in Japanese Language Study and Learners' Cultural/Linguistics Backgrounds. *Australian Review of Applied Linguistics*, 32 (2): 10.1–10.17.

Mercer, S. (2011), *Towards an Understanding of Language Learner Self-Concept*, New York: Springer.

Mercer, S. (2015), 'Dynamics of the Self: A Multilevel Nested Systems Approach', in Z. Dörnyei, P. MacIntyre and A. Henry (eds), *Motivational Dynamics in Language Learning*, 139–63, Bristol: Multilingual Matters.

Mercer, S. and M. Williams (2014), 'Introduction', in S. Mercer and M. Williams (eds), *Multiple Perspectives on the Self in SLA*, 1–5, Bristol: Multilingual Matters.

Mills, N. (2014), 'Self-Esteem and Self-Concept in Foreign Language Learning', in S. Mercer and M. Williams (eds), *Multiple Perspectives on the Self in SLA*, 7–22, Bristol: Multilingual Matters.

Mowrer, O. H. (1950), *Learning Theory and Personality Dynamics*, New York: Ronald.

Murray, G., X. Gao and T. Lamb (2011), *Identity, Motivation and Autonomy in Language Learning*, Bristol: Multilingual Matters.

Nakamura, T. (2015), 'Motivation for Learning Japanese and Other Additional Languages: A Study of L2 Self-Images Across Multiple Languages', *New Voices in Japanese Studies*, 7: 39–58.

Nemoto, A. (2011), 'カタールにおける日本語学習動機に関する一考察: LTI 日本語講座修了者へのインタビュー調査から', 一橋大学国際教育センター紀要, 2: 85–96.

Nishitani, M. (2009), '動機づけ・外国語不安の捉え方と学習方略：ベトナムと中国の学習者の比較', 一橋大学国際教育センター紀要, 12: 15–25.

Northwood, B. M. (2013), 'Passion and Persistence: A Study of Motivation among Learners of Japanese in Australia', PhD diss., University of New South Wales, Sydney.

Northwood, B. M. and C. K. Thomson (2012), 'What Keeps Them Going? Investigating Ongoing Learners of Japanese in Australian Universities', *Japanese Studies*, 32 (3): 335–55.

Nuibe, Y., F. Kano and K. Ito (1995), '大学生の日本語学習動機に関する国際調査—ニュージーランドの場合—', 日本語教育, 86: 162–72.

Ortega, L. (2016), 'Multi-Competence in Second Language Acquisition: Inroads into the Mainstream?', in V. Cook and W. Li (eds), *The Cambridge Handbook of Linguistic Multicompetence*, 50–76, Cambridge: Cambridge University Press.

Oyserman, D. (2007), 'Social Identity and Self-Regulation', in A. W. Kruglanski and E. T. Higgins (eds), *Social Psychology: Handbook of Basic Principles*, 432–53, New York: Guilford Press.

Oyserman, D., D. Bybee and K. Terry (2006), 'Possible Selves and Academic Outcomes: How and When Possible Selves Impel Action', *Journal of Personality and Social Psychology*, 91 (1): 188–204.

Oyserman, D., D. Bybee., K. Terry and T. Hart-Johnson (2004), 'Possible Selves as Roadmaps', *Journal of Research in Personality*, 38: 130–49.

Oyserman, D. and S. Fryberg (2006), 'The Possible Selves of Diverse Adolescents: Content and Function Across Gender, Race and National Origin', in C. Dunkel and J. Kerpelman (eds), *Possible Selves: Theory, Research, and Applications*, 17–39, New York: Nova Science Publishers.

Oyserman, D. and L. James (2009), 'Possible Selves: From Content to Process', in W. Markman, W. M. P. Klein and J. A. Suhr (eds), *The Handbook of Imagination and Mental Stimulation*, 373–94, New York: Psychology Press.

Oyserman, D. and H. Markus (1990), 'Possible Selves and Delinquency', *Journal of Personality and Social Psychology*, 59 (1): 112–25.

Park, J. S-Y. (2009), *The Local Construction of a Global Language: Ideologies of English in South Korea*, Berlin: Mouton de Gruyter.

Pavlenko, A. (2006), *Bilingual Minds: Emotional Experience, Expression and Representation*, Bristol: Multilingual Matters.

Quinlan, S. L., J. Jaccard and H. Blanton (2006), 'A Decision Theoretic and Prototype Conceptualization of Possible Selves: Implications for the Prediction of Risk Behavior', *Journal of Personality*, 74 (2): 599–630.

Richards, K. (2003), *Qualitative Inquiry in TESOL*, Basingstoke: Palgrave Macmillan.

Romaine, S. (1989), *Bilingualism*, Oxford: Blackwell.

Rubio, F. D. (2014), 'Self-Esteem and Self-Concept in Foreign Language Learning', in S. Mercer and M. Williams (eds), *Multiple Perspectives on the Self in SLA*, 41–58, Bristol: Multilingual Matters.

Ryan, R. M. and E. L. Deci (2003), 'On Assimilating Identities to the Self: A Self-Determination Theory Perspective on Internalization and Integrity within Cultures', in M. R. Leary and J. P. Tangney (eds), *Handbook of Self and Identity*, 253–72, New York: Guilford Press.

Sampasivam, S. and R. Clément (2014), 'The Dynamics of Second Language Confidence: Contact and Interaction', in S. Mercer and M. Williams (eds), *Multiple Perspectives on the Self in SLA*, 23–40, Bristol: Multilingual Matters.

Schmidt, G. (2014), 'Personal Growth as a Strong Element in the Motivation of Australian University Students to Learn German', *Australian Review of Applied Linguistics*, 37 (2): 145–60.

Siegal, M. (1996), 'The Role of Learner Subjectivity in Second Language Sociolinguistic Competency: Western Women Learning Japanese', *Applied Linguistics*, 17 (3): 356–82.

Unemori, P., H. Omoregie and H. Markus (2004), 'Self-Portraits: Possible Selves in European-American, Chilean, Japanese and Japanese-American Cultural Contexts', *Self and Identity*, 3 (4): 321–38.

Ushioda, E. (1998), 'Effective Motivational Thinking: A Cognitive Theoretical Approach to the Study of Language Learning Motivation', in E. A. Soler and V. C.

Espurz (eds), *Current Issues in English Language Methodology*, 77–90, Castelló de la Plana: Universitat Jaume.

Ushioda, E. (2009), 'A Person-in-Context Relational View of Emergent Motivation, Self and Identity', in Z. Dörnyei and E. Ushioda (eds), *Motivation, Language Identity and the L2 Self*, 215–28, Bristol: Multilingual Matters.

Ushioda, E. (2017), 'The Impact of Global English on Motivation to Learn Other Languages: Toward an Ideal Multilingual Self', *The Modern Language Journal*, 101 (3): 469–82.

Ushioda, E and Z. Dörnyei, eds (2017), 'Beyond Global English: Motivation to Learn Languages in a Multicultural World', *The Modern Language Journal*, 101 (3): 449–607.

Van Geert, P. (2008), 'The Dynamic Systems Approach in the Study of L1 and L2 Acquisition: An Introduction', *The Modern Language Journal*, 92 (2): 179–99.

Verspoor, M. (2015), 'Initial Conditions', in Z. Dörnyei, P. MacIntyre and A. Henry (eds), *Motivational Dynamics in Language Learning*, 38–46, Bristol: Multilingual Matters.

Waninge, F. (2015), 'Motivation, Emotion and Cognition: Attractor States in the Classroom', in Z. Dörnyei, P. MacIntyre and A. Henry (eds), *Motivational Dynamics in Language Learning*, 195–213, Bristol: Multilingual Matters.

You, C. J., Z. Dörnyei and K. Csizér (2015), 'Motivation, Vision, and Gender: A Survey of Learners of English in China', *Language Learning*, 66 (1): 94–123.

Zaragoza, E. D. C. (2011), 'Identity, Motivation and Plurilingualism in Self-Access Centers', in G. Murray, X. Gao and T. Lamb (eds), *Identity, Motivation and Autonomy in Language Learning*, 91–106, Bristol: Multilingual Matters.

Index

academic credentials 33, 40, 42, 50, 86, 92, 95, 99, 101, 122
academic goals 98, 100, 102, 118
actual self 17, 120
Al-Hoorie, A. H. 134
attractor state 123, 126, 130
　Korean learners and 87, 93, 95, 96, 98, 99, 101, 102
Australian Academy of the Humanities 5
Australian learners
　background of 51–4
　Japanese as primary language for 71–6
　Japanese learning experience 54–5
　　cultural and social influences 55–6, 57–8, 60, 61, 64, 65–7
　　educational influences 56–7, 62–4
　　goals 58–9, 68–9
　　ideal Japanese self 67–8
　　university study 58–65
　learning experiences 69–71, 105–8
　motivational dynamics 112–14
　shift in perceived future use of languages 108–11
　sustained motivational trajectory 114–15
　　case studies 115–23
　waning motivational trajectory 123
　　case study 123–31

Bakhtin, M. M. 149
balanced possible selves 20
bilingualism 22–4, 27, 30, 51, 119, 128, 131, 134, 141, 142, 144, 146, 147
　complementarity principle of 23
　identities 24
　motivation 24–6
Block, D. 24
Bybee, D. 18

career
　demands for English as language for 88, 93, 96, 99, 102, 103, 126, 131, 140, 148 (*see also* Korean learners)

domain 8, 9, 39, 40, 43, 45, 50, 134, 139, 141, 148
　Australian learners' motivational trajectories 108, 116, 122–4, 126, 129, 130
　Australian learners' motivation and future self-images and 68, 69, 72, 75, 76
　Korean learners' motivational trajectories and 86, 91, 92, 96, 102
future 8, 34, 49, 67, 68, 75, 91, 97–101, 114, 116–17, 124, 145, 147
Chan, L. 25
Chen, S. W. 4
Clément, R. 13
coadaptation and system parameter 96, 103, 118–19, 122, 123, 131, 134, 141, 143, 146
　competition 144–5
comparative research 4
complementarity principle 23, 144
Cook, V. 150
cooperative L2 selves 49, 75–6
core personality traits 16
Csizér, K. 12, 25, 26, 134, 144
cultural influences 4, 5, 14, 19, 22, 24, 28, 123, 131
　Australian learners' motivation and future self-images and 51, 54, 55, 61, 63, 64, 69, 71, 76
　language-learning motivation in English- and non-English-speaking contexts 137, 143, 144, 149–51
current self/self-system 17, 19, 75, 93, 113, 118, 120–2, 126, 130
　language-learning motivation in English- and non-English-speaking contexts and 135, 136, 138, 139, 142, 145–8, 150, 153

De Bot, K. 28, 146
Deci, E. L. 139

demands for bilingual native speakers of English 131, 141, 146, 147
demands for English as a career language 88, 93, 96, 99, 102, 103, 126, 131, 140, 148
domain of possible selves, concept of 4, 15, 27, 43, 133
domain specificity 22–3
Dörnyei, Z. 1, 4, 12, 13, 25, 26, 27, 28, 134, 139, 142, 144, 154
Dunkel, C. S. 19
Dynamic Model of Multilingualism (DMM) 21–2
dynamic systems theory (DST) 21, 28
  Australian learners' motivational trajectories and 113, 118, 122–3, 126, 130, 131
  Korean learners' motivational trajectories and 79, 87, 92, 95, 96, 98, 101, 103
  language learning motivation in English- and non-English- speaking contexts and 135, 139, 140, 143, 145–8

English learning experience, of Korean learners 41–3
Japanese as preliminary language to English
  cooperative L2 selves 49
  L2 self domain 43–6
  pressure not to study Japanese and study English 46–8
English motivational system 96, 99, 101, 126
expected self 17, 20

feared self 17, 20
  L2 136–7
feared self-image 64
fixed attractor 144
Fryberg, S. 16
functional differentiation, within multilingual language system 22–3
future self-concept 30, 43, 45
future self-guides 16–18, 39–40, 46, 49, 64, 71, 87, 134
future self-image 30, 32, 37, 39, 40, 45, 49, 71, 86, 93, 95, 114, 117

future self-representation 34, 76, 139

Gardner, R. C. 1, 3, 11, 12, 13, 14, 27
Global English impact 140–2
goals 32, 43, 47, 68, 70, 75, 86, 88–92, 98, 103, 108, 114, 116–25, 147, 152, 153
  academic 98, 100, 102, 118
  alternative 38, 93, 94, 95, 135
  attainment of 38–9, 135–6
  cognitive 8, 45, 72
  extrinsic/external 36–8, 50, 65, 99–100, 150
  internal 150, 151
  long-term 38, 39, 48, 50, 58–9, 77, 140, 141, 148
  multiple 26, 48
  short-term 33–5, 39, 40, 42, 48, 143, 149
  subsidiary 113, 120, 121
  ultimate 94, 116, 120, 121, 143
  visions and 45
Grosjean, F. 23, 24, 144

Henry, A. 2, 25, 26, 103, 144
Herdina, P. 21, 22
Higgins, E. T. 16, 17, 18
hoped-for self 17
Hosokawa, H. 150
Hoyle, R. H. 20, 34
Hsu, C. C. 4
Huang, H. T. 4
hybrid self-concept 24

ideal/ought self. *See* future self-guides
ideal English self-image 15, 26
ideal English self/self-system 89, 93, 101, 126, 127
ideal Japanese self 9, 15, 32, 58, 88, 92–6, 98, 100, 101, 111, 113, 122, 135, 136, 146–8
  development of 39–40, 67–8
Ideal Japanese self-image 62, 69, 88, 101, 128, 130, 137, 138
ideal Japanese self-system 93, 95, 98, 101, 118, 122, 127, 130, 131, 135, 146
ideal L2 self 13, 64, 122, 125
  achievement 135–6
  constructing 66

ideal multilingual self/self-system 26, 103, 122, 123, 130, 134, 143, 153
  construction of 142–4
ideal multilingual self-image 91, 131
ideal self-image 37, 59, 66, 75, 76, 93, 98, 113, 118, 122, 126, 142–3, 149. *See also* ideal English self-image; ideal Japanese self-image
ideal self-representation 62, 66
identification, concept of 11–12
identity and self-concept 16
independent study (self-study) 32–3, 93
institutional settings, language learners in 48. *See also* Australian learners
integrative motivation 13, 138
integrativeness, concept of 12
interpersonal domain 39, 45, 69, 71, 72, 81, 98, 101, 129, 138, 139, 150

James, L. 27
Japanese as foreign language (JFL) learners 15
Japanese as second language (JSL) learners 15
Japanese-Language Proficiency Test (JLPT) (Korea) 7, 89, 92, 120, 124, 135
  motivation and future self-images and 33, 34, 35, 38, 40
Japanese motivational system 28, 135, 139, 146, 147
  Australian learners and 113, 118, 122, 126, 130
  Koreans learners and 92, 93, 95–6, 98, 101
Japanese Proficiency Test (JPT) (Korea) 7, 38, 92, 97
Japan Exchange and Teaching (JET) Program 81, 108, 113, 116, 120, 141
Japan Foundation, The 5
Jessner, U. 21, 22

Kanno, Y. 24
Korea, Japanese language learning motivation in 15
Korean learners 29
  background of 29–30, 31
  English learning experience of 41–3

Japanese as preliminary language to English
  cooperative L2 selves 49
  L2 self domain 43–6
  pressure not to study Japanese and study English 46–8
Japanese learning experience and attainment of goals 38–9
  extrinsic goals 36–8
  ideal Japanese self development 39–40
  initial motivation to study Japanese at university 35–6
  intentions to continue studying Japanese 40–1
  Japanese as short-term goal 33–5
  Japanese pop culture interest 30, 32
  self-study 32–3
language learning experience 79–86
motivational dynamics for 87–8
shifts in perceived future use of languages for 86–7
sustained motivational trajectory of 88–9
  case studies 89–96
waning motivational trajectory for 96–7
  case studies 97–102
Kormos, J. 134

L1 acquisition 11
L2 language/culture interest 138–40
L2 learning experience 13, 27, 29, 48, 51, 76, 89, 114, 137–8, 145, 146, 150
L2 Motivational Self System 1, 2, 4, 9, 12–13, 15, 16, 27–9, 138, 149, 151, 154
L2 self-concept 23, 43–6, 49, 122, 134, 136, 71–2, 73, 150
L2 self-guide 28, 58, 69, 150
L2 selves, *see individual entries*
L3 selves 2, 25, 48, 49, 75, 93, 122, 123, 130, 142–5, 151. *See also* Australian learners; Korean learners
L4 selves 30, 49, 74, 75, 93, 115, 122, 123, 130, 135, 142–5, 151
Lambert, W. E. 1, 11, 12, 13
language learner, significance of 28
language learning motivation 133. *See also individual entries*

across multiple languages
　competition and coadaptation 144–5
　Global English impact 140–2
　ideal multilingual self
　　construction 142–4
　future research suggestions 151–4
　motivation to learn LOTE
　　feared L2 self 136–7
　　ideal L2 self achievement 135–6
　　L2 language/culture interest 138–40
　　L2 learning experience 137–8
　　L2 self domain 133–5
　practical implications 149–51
　sustained motivational trajectory
　　signature dynamics 145–7
　waning motivational trajectory
　　signature dynamics 147–8
language other than English
　(LOTE) 5, 133
　motivation to learn
　　feared L2 self 136–7
　　ideal L2 self achievement 135–6
　　L2 language/culture interest 138–40
　　L2 learning experience 137–8
　　L2 self domain 133–5
Lanvers, U. 141
Lee, S. H. 15
leisure domain 39, 43, 50, 76, 81, 94, 98,
　122, 123, 126
　language learning motivation and 134,
　　135, 138, 141, 146, 147, 150
leisure interests, influence on motivation
　8, 69, 98, 99, 101, 114, 121, 122
Leung, C. 151
linguistic capital 140
long-term goals 38, 39, 48, 50, 58–9, 77,
　140, 141, 148
long-term future self 35
Lowie, W. 28
Lukács, G. 26
Lyons, D. 48, 150

MacIntyre, P. D. 13
MacKinnon, S. P. 13
Mandarin 25, 30, 34, 47, 71, 75, 89–93,
　103, 121, 123, 130, 143
Markus, H. 16, 17–18, 27, 134, 154
Matsumoto, M. 14, 64, 69
Mercer, S. 16, 23, 24, 99

Modern Language Journal, The 26, 142
monolingual bias 2
monolingualism 5, 6, 22, 24, 51, 63, 137,
　141, 143, 151
motivation, for learning Japanese
　14–15. *See also* language learning
　motivation
motivational decline 100
motivational dynamics 87–8, 108, 112–14
Mowrer, O. H. 13
multi-competence 144
　linguistic 150
multilingualism 3, 20–1. *See also*
　individual entries
　bi/multilingual identities 23–4
　bi/multilingual motivation 24–6
　conceptual frameworks 27–8
　domain of language behaviour 22–3
　Dynamic Model of Multilingualism
　　(DMM) 21–2
　identities 23–4

Nakamura, T. 15
National Policy on Languages (Australia) 5
non-native languages 3
Northwood, B. M. 14, 130
Nurius, P. 16, 17–18, 134, 154

Omoregie, H. 27
Ortega, L. 144
ought-to self
　English self 43, 50, 96, 99, 126
　Japanese self 100
　L2 self 13
　representation 37
Oyserman, D. 16, 18, 27

Park, J. S-Y. 140
Pavlenko, A. 24, 142
personality traits, core 16
pop culture 14, 15
　Australian learners and 55–6, 60, 61, 65,
　　71, 76, 111, 114, 123, 125–6, 131
　Korean learners and 30, 32, 34, 35, 36,
　　50, 81, 86, 87, 96–9, 101
　language learning motivation and 134,
　　136, 138–9, 147, 150
possible selves 15, 42
　feared self and 20

and future self-guides 16–18
generation, achievement, and elimination of 19–20
self and self-concept and 15–16
as social constructions 18–19
Possible Selves Theory 12

repeller state 93, 95, 101, 126, 136
research contexts 4–5
   Australia 5–6
   data gathering and analysis 7–9
   Korea 6–7
   participants 7
Richards, K. 8
Ryan, R. M. 139

Scarino, A. 151
Schmidt, G. 5
self-concept, significance of
   current 26, 40, 93, 115, 120–2, 135, 136
   future 30, 40, 43, 45, 154
   hybrid 24, 142
   significance of 12, 13, 16, 17, 23–4, 43, 49, 126, 134, 139, 150
   working 25–6
self-confidence, of learners 60, 92, 108, 115, 122, 124, 128, 130
Self-Discrepancy Theory 12, 17
self-organization 103
short-term goals 33–5, 39, 40, 42, 48, 143, 149
short-term future self 35, 40

Socio-educational (SE) model of language acquisition 3, 11–14, 27, 138
Sherrill, M. R. 20, 34
Siegal, M. 137
speech genres 149
sustained motivational trajectory 88–9, 112, 114–15
   case studies 89–96, 115–23
   signature dynamics in 145–7
system parameters 96, 99, 102–3, 140

Terry, K. 18
Test of English for International Communication (TOEIC) (Korea) 7, 42, 95
Thomson, C. K. 14, 130

Unemori, P. 27
university study 4, 5, 28, 29, 43, 64, 66, 79, 87, 88, 93, 94, 101, 102, 130
Ushioda, E. 24, 26, 27, 48, 60, 139, 142

Verspoor, M. 28
Victoria Certificate of Education (VCE) 63

Waninge, F. 139
waning motivational trajectory 88, 96–7, 113
   case studies 97–102, 123–31
   signature dynamics in 147–8
working self-concept 25–6

www.ingramcontent.com/pod-product-compliance
Lightning Source LLC
Chambersburg PA
CBHW052046300426
44117CB00012B/1998